Jim's Path

Jim's Path

A Story of God's Unfailing Faithfulness
to One Family

James D. Fritz & Irma Jane Zager

Pleasant Word
A Division of WINEPRESS PUBLISHING

Printed in the United States of America

Packaged by Pleasant Word, a division of WinePress Publishing, PO Box 428, Enumclaw, WA 98022. The views expressed or implied in this work do not necessarily reflect those of Pleasant Word, a division of WinePress Publishing. Ultimate design, content, and editorial accuracy of this work are the responsibilities of the author.

Unless otherwise noted, all Scriptures are taken from the King James Version of the Bible.

Scripture references marked NKJ are taken from the New King James Version, Copyright © 1979, 1980, 1982 by Thomas Nelson, Inc., Publishers. Used by permission.

Scripture references marked NASB are taken from the New American Standard Bible, © 1960, 1963, 1968, 1971, 1972, 1973, 1975, 1977 by The Lockman Foundation. Used by permission.

ISBN 1-57921-615-3
Library of Congress Catalog Card Number: 2003101734

Table of Contents

Introduction

Here we are, a mother and her son, both caught in the down-spiraling winds of tragedy. We tell our story because we want to give glory to God who was so faithful to bring us through it all. In the process, He burnt out the dross and changed us into better people. He also changed many others along the way. We tell our story so you can know that God can cause ". . . all things to work together for good to them that love God . . ." (Romans 8:28). Not only did He change tragedy into triumph; but also He brought strength out of weakness and happiness out of great sorrow. God is so good. He is so faithful. He is so loving.

In 1980, I was involved in an automobile accident. I became a quadriplegic and was confined to a wheelchair. My life was changed forever. This is my story, *Jim's Path*.

It has been a tremendous blessing for me to review my life in a wheelchair and how God has provided for my needs every step of the way. It has also caused me to relive some of the most painful experiences and emotions of my life during those difficult days following my accident. I hope that it will be a blessing to others.

The purpose for writing my testimony is to be an encouragement to others who are suffering from adversity. That includes pretty much everyone. In seeking to encourage others I hope to communicate three truths that have been very powerfully etched into the fabric of my life. First, God is good! Whatever the circumstances, difficulties, or trials, God wants to use them to draw us closer to Him and His will for our lives. He loves His children and wants to see them grow in the grace and knowledge of our Lord Jesus Christ. Second, God can still use you! After my accident, I struggled a great deal with being useful. I didn't like feeling that I was a burden all the time. I wanted to have purpose in my life. I hope that my testimony is an example of how God can enable even the handicapped to be productive and fruitful for the Lord Jesus Christ. I hope that it will provide the motivation for someone to persevere in overcoming adversity. And third, life can still be fulfilling. I can't express in words the joy, peace, and contentment that I have in my life today. That doesn't mean that I am free from struggles, but I praise God for His goodness to me. I have a wonderful wife and daughter, a ministry that I love very much, and I am surrounded by friends and family who are a tremendous encouragement to me every step of the way.

Another purpose for writing my testimony is because there is a great deal of unbiblical teaching in the church today about suffering. It has misled many and has even destroyed the faith of some. My burden as a fundamentalist Christian is to portray God's teaching from His Word accurately. My desire is for people to see the manifold grace of God even in the midst of adversity. My hope is that people will see suffering as an opportunity to glorify God.

I would like to say one more thing. It is so easy for us to fix our eyes on people instead of the Lord Jesus Christ. My desire is that the Lord be glorified through my testimony. I want to be an example of what God can do, not what I can do. May God be glorified through His marvelous demonstration of grace in my life!

Note: The non-italicized text refers to Jim's testimony and *the italicized text refers to Mom's testimony.*

For Our Light Affliction

Why Me?

Everyone asks this question sometime in life. The combination of curiosity, heartbreak, fear, and lifelong dreams make the "Why me?" question a natural response to difficult circumstances. I can remember vividly the scene in my life when "Why me?" etched itself indelibly in my mind. At the time I was still a patient at a VA facility in the Midwest. I was 19 years old and just coming to grips with the fact that I would spend the rest of my life in a wheelchair, paralyzed from the shoulders down. I was in a hospital full of Vietnam vets and World War II vets. I was young, I felt alone, and I was scared. One late afternoon, sitting by myself in the recreation room on the tenth floor, I looked out the big picture window to the freeway below. As the minutes ticked away, thousands of people drove by, completely unaware that I was watching them; and of all those people, not one knew I was there. Not one understood what I was going through. Not one even seemed to care. Thousands of people whose lives were going on while my life was falling apart before my very eyes.

It was then that the big question, "Why me?" burst into my mind with a force that I cannot begin to describe; it can only be experienced. I looked up to God with tears in my eyes and anger in my heart, and said, "God, of all these thousands of people, why me? Why did You choose to put me in this wheelchair? I don't like it and I don't want it, and as long as I'm here I cannot and will not serve you!"

Now these are some pretty bold words to shout into the face of an almighty and sovereign God, but that's the way I felt. I didn't like the direction my life was taking and I wanted God to change it. I knew that He could if He wanted to, and I was demanding that He do so.

Why me? I didn't ask God the question just that way. I asked, "Why my son, God? Why my good, beautiful son? Why not me? Why not one of those longhaired, loser kids I see smoking pot, drinking, driving fast, disobeying the law and cursing God? Why can they swagger jauntily down the street while my dear child lies helpless and unable to move anything but his head?" "Why not me, Lord. Or why not someone else?"

I didn't demand as Jim did, but I begged and groveled on my knees. "I know you have the power, Lord. Why don't you do it?" Because I wanted it so badly, I was sure that Jim's healing must be God's will and it would happen sometime. Even today, twenty years later, I know God will do it when He's ready. One day I will again see my son, tall and straight as the Lord meant him to be.

Jim's dad also asked the "Why me?" question in a different way. He, with even more vehemence, asked, "Why not me!" He ranted and raved and shook his fist at the God he had so recently learned to love. His reaction was very angry, but God was certainly real to him. God was a person and He was doing things that Doug, my husband, didn't like. He reacted as he would have to any real physical person. He loved God and God had not pleased him. He did not take time to think. He loved his son and God had allowed him to be terribly hurt. Jim's dad had many faults, as we all do, but there was never a man who loved his children more than he did. They were more than his life and he would gladly have given his life for them.

Before I go on, I believe it would be helpful to take you back to who I was before that fateful day on October 29, 1980. I grew up in a typical, middle-class home in Medina, a small town in Northeast Ohio. I had a mom and dad, two brothers and one sister. And besides the typical sibling rivalries, we were a very close-knit family. I loved the outdoors and pretty much anything that had to do with sports. I had been water skiing

since the age of 7; I played football, wrestled, and ran track from junior high on. As a family we would often take trips to the western United States. One of our favorite activities was hiking in the Rocky Mountains, sometimes taking day trips and at other times staying overnight. My folks had a summer home in Canada where I spent every summer from the time I was 4 years old. Those days were filled with skiing, swimming, tree fort building, and playing kick-the-can, hide-n-seek, and all kinds of other fun activities. I learned to love the outdoors. I learned to love competition. I learned to love adventure.

Our family was middle class, middle income, middle America, middle, middle, middle—. To tell our story is to tell the stories of families all across the nation. We were God-fearing, mor-

ally upright, sometimes church-going, community serving, law-abiding, fiercely patriotic, backbone citizens of the United States of America. We would have called ourselves good Christian people.

My husband, Doug, was a strong-willed, adventurous man who loved his family and made it the center of his life. He came home every night right after work. He spent hours on the school ground supporting his children's activities. On payday, he turned his check over to me for the family use. If he had ever signed it himself, it probably would have been refused at the bank as a forgery. He was the head of our household and a strong disciplinarian who believed in the value of hard work. He got angry over small transgressions; but when the children got in serious trouble, his first question was always "Are you hurt?"

Jim was the third child in a family of four. His two older siblings were brother John, the eldest and sister Jackie. He had a younger brother, Jensen, who was always called JD. All of our children were greatly loved and wanted. Each child seemed as precious as the other did. I loved them with a mother's love that only a mother can appreciate. They were my life.

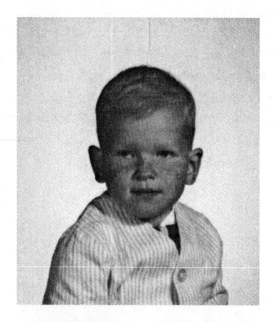

Jim was no exception to that. When he was born, he was pure pleasure and I thanked God for such a darling child. He had the bluest eyes, beautiful red hair, freckles everywhere, a sturdy, chubby little body, the sunniest smile ever, and alto-

gether he was an adorable child. During emotional times I remembered God and I did thank Him for the wonderful blessing of children and family.

For the most part though, we were too busy enjoying the provision of God's blessings to stop and really think about Him. We had heard the Gospel, but it had no real meaning for us. We didn't really understand.

When I was in the fourth grade, my older brother, John, received an appointment to the United States Air Force Academy. That summer, our family took a trip to Colorado Springs, Colorado to see him. I can remember my dad's pride that his son was a cadet at USAFA. Through the eyes of a nine-year old, everything I saw was absolutely fascinating. Soldiers marching in formation with rifles, obstacle courses, and the beautiful Mountains that surrounded the Academy captured my imagination. I was hooked. I wanted to be a cadet too. And from that time on, I set my sights on that goal.

Because the Academy was so selective, I knew that I had to excel in a number of different areas in order to receive an appointment. Academics, student leadership activities, and athletics were all very important ingredients. But with my goal firmly fixed in my heart I forged ahead with determination. I concentrated on academics and I got involved in as many activities as I could. And even though these things took a lot of my time, it didn't detract from my social life. In fact, most of what I was involved in enhanced my social status and it made me very popular. My life in those days was pretty good and everything seemed to be going my way.

It wasn't until the summer after my sophomore year in high school that the first significant trial came into my life. My dad was diagnosed with cancer. Though it was a devastating and scary turn of events, the prognosis for my dad was good. He underwent surgery to remove a kidney and the doctors were quite confident that they had gotten it all. It was during this time that Dad started doing some serious soul searching, and God provided a special couple to be His ambassadors to my family. Jim and Dawn Imig were my folks' best friends, and it just so happened that I was dating their daughter, Kim, at the same time. God was working on two fronts. The thing that struck me the most about the Imigs was the change in their lives. They had just recently been saved themselves and had come into a personal relationship with Jesus Christ. We could see the dynamic difference it had made. They were excited about serving Jesus. Their newfound belief meant something to them. Of course, I noticed it mostly in Kim. She started carrying a Bible around in school, and in a public school that was a pretty strange thing. One day she asked me if I wanted to go to a Wednesday night Bible study. "Bible study!" I exclaimed. "I don't need the Bible. I go to church on Sunday and that's enough." But she was persistent, pretty, and persuasive, and I was 17 and in love, so finally I went.

That night changed my life forever. You see, I thought I was a good person. I went to church. I didn't do bad things (at least things that I thought were bad). I tried to be a good, upstanding citizen. But that night, I was shown things out of the Bible I had never been told before. I was a sinner. I was alienated from God and I was His enemy. And, worst of all, there was nothing in and of myself that I could do about it. Then they told me the good news. Jesus Christ died for my sins. He rose again that I might have new life. And all that I had to do to care for my sin problem was confess my sin and accept what Jesus Christ did for me on the cross. I had never heard anything like that before, but I knew it was true.

For the next three months I searched the Scriptures, went to that little country church as often as I could, and grappled with what I was going to do with Jesus Christ. I know that I was the object of much prayer and intense witnessing. One night as I was getting ready to leave Kim's house, Kim's parents, Kim and I sat down to pray. That was something they did every night before I left. I thank the Lord for it now, but at the time it seemed like a pretty strange thing to do. That night God was working on my heart. I knew it was time to make a decision. I was either going to follow Christ wholeheartedly, or have nothing to do with Him at all. I can remember it so clearly. We were all sitting in a circle and they prayed around until it was my turn. Then I prayed and accepted Jesus Christ as my Savior, and immediately the burden of sin was lifted. I was a new creature in Christ. That same week my dad accepted the Lord as his Savior. Shortly after that my younger brother was saved. About three months after that my sister trusted in Christ. And some time subsequent to that my mom committed herself to Christ also. It was a dramatic change in our family. Praise God for His saving grace!

What a change is right! Change often is accompanied by a great deal of pain and I experienced it all! The Imigs were close, dear friends of the whole family and when they left our social, mainline church to go to this little, nothing place out in the country; I felt like they were traitors. Then, to make matters worse, they enticed my husband to go to their Bible studies. Doug, my husband of nearly thirty years, got very intrigued with these studies and I thought he had lost it. Jesus was someone I said I believed in; but I rarely gave thought to Him. Religion was a private thing; prayers were said sometimes at night and sometimes at the table when you remembered, and when troubles came that were too big to be handled by yourself. Now here was my spouse talking about loving God and being "born again"! These were the days of the Jesus freaks and my son and my husband were becoming like them. I just hoped they would get tired of this foolishness and get back to normal soon.

Never belittle the power of prayer. Only because of the prayers and faithfulness of my husband, Jim, the Imigs, and the church, was the wall surrounding my heart and my mind removed. I finally went to their church. It was under duress and accompanied by my tears. It was Easter Sunday and if I wanted to spend it with my husband and my sons, I would have to give in and go to church with them. JD loved the new church and its young peoples' group. John and Jackie were gone from home by now. I still remember sitting in church, wiping the tears away and feeling sorry for myself because my family cared so little for my happiness that they couldn't go to church with ME. Praise the Lord that they were adamant. I went that Easter Sunday and I heard the Gospel message. I also saw a church that was really alive. These people lived their beliefs and they had something I wanted—Christ's love.

After becoming a Christian, life settled down again. My dad's cancer was in remission. Everyone was healthy. I was doing well in school and in sports. God was blessing me. I won the district track meet in pole-vaulting and qualified for the State Track and Field Championship my senior year. I had a girlfriend. And I fulfilled my lifelong dream—I received an appointment to the United States Air Force Academy. I graduated from high school in June of 1979 and before the month was over I was off to basic training at the Academy. After that, things continued to go well and I thought that this Christianity was pretty good stuff. God was certainly blessing the Fritzes. Dad's cancer remained in remission and I was having good success at the Academy. My first year, I was one of only two freshman who made the varsity track team. I was passing all my classes and I loved the military atmosphere. God gave me a good, Christian roommate. I found lots of fellowship among other cadets and local churches. And I was surrounded by some of the most beautiful country in the United States.

As it turns out, I can see that my days at the Academy were definitely a time of preparation for what was to come. The discipline and submission to authority that I learned as I was going through the 4th class training has become an invaluable part of my life. Very early on in the training, we learned we had three responses that we could give any time we were addressed by an upper classman. They were "Yes Sir," "No Sir," or "No Excuse, Sir!" For that entire year we were indoctrinated with the concept of submitting to authority. That sure has come in handy as I attempt to submit my life to the will of God. I was also prepared through all the physical challenges. Obstacle courses, basic training, morning runs, and daily marches taught me how to endure and persevere. And, God was kind to allow me to do some things that most people never have the opportunity to do. I got to parachute, fly sail planes (an airplane that had no engine), ski practically free of charge in the Rocky Mountains, and go through different types of training that stretched me mentally and physically beyond anything that I could have ever imagined.

Jim was not the only one being prepared for what was to come. God's foresight never ceases to amaze me, though why I should be amazed at God's greatness, I don't know. It's just that his planning is so far beyond anything I can imagine.

God was preparing me years before when the last child had reached Junior High School. I found I needed something more fulfilling than bridge and shopping while the children were away; so I began substitute teaching at the local high school. It was not a job that brought much satisfaction because you never get to do your own thing. You follow someone else's teaching plan and their method of delivery as best you can. However, I got to know the faculty and the administration. When the need arose for a Learning Disability Program at the high school level, they thought of me.

Another young teacher and myself were to implement the program. Rich Clevidence, my colleague, was in a wheelchair. He was paralyzed from the neck down as a result of a diving accident when he was just 18. Nevertheless, he was one of the most dynamic teachers I have ever encountered. The wheelchair never prevented him from doing his job with excellence. Moreover, he was a tremendous encouragement to our handicapped students.

Together we served the students all day and then at night we tooled off together to Akron University to get certified for what we were doing. Rich became a really close friend and I learned so much from him. Particularly I learned that a wheelchair doesn't mean non-productivity. For Rich the wheelchair limited him only in physical ability. Nothing else was beyond him. Rich taught me that life is an attitude; but especially it is a gift. Life for Rich, even in a wheelchair was full and happy. God wanted me to know that. He planned that I would have that knowledge before I knew I needed it. Our God is so great!

God was preparing us in other ways too. All of the family at home was going to a home Bible study, Wednesday night prayer and study, Sunday school Bible study, and Pastor Wolfe's wonderful teaching in church. We were eager to learn and our little church was there to teach us God's word. We didn't realize then how much we would need His wonderful promises. We were changing too. Jim's dad, who used to be able to turn the air blue with his cursing when things didn't go just right; no longer ever took the Lord's name in vain. Not once, after he was saved, did he utter any of the words that were always labeled "Dad's words." These were inevitably heard by the children; but they knew they were not words they could use. Doug changed in more ways than speech too. He grew softer and more sensitive to others and no longer seemed controlled by anger. He was a much easier man to live with after he knew the Lord. I am sure I changed too, but recognizing change in oneself is not so easy. I know that I had a desire to please God that I had never had before.

The diagnosis of renal cancer in Doug's kidney shook us to the core. We had always been such an active, healthy family. We were proud of our physical well being. Nevertheless, we now had the Lord in our lives. He would take care of us. Doug went in to the Cleveland Clinic to have the cancerous kidney removed and the Doctor seemed confidant that he had gotten all the cancer. We praised the Lord for His wonderful provision in our lives.

Jumping out of a perfectly good, flight-worthy, safe, no-reason-to-jump-out-of airplane was not my idea of fun. I had just finished my freshmen year, and I was looking forward to some activities with less intensity. As I checked out the summer assignments, much to my surprise I was listed for something that I had never really even considered. But there it was—AM 490 (Airmanship 490). What a surprise! Only the top cadets academically were chosen for this program (and I was nowhere near the top). But, I was going to get to jump out of a perfectly good airplane 5 times at 4,500 feet with nothing between the law of gravity and me but a thin piece of nylon material. That's right! I was chosen for the Free-Fall Parachute Program.

At first, I thought that this was a pretty cool idea. I went through the training phase of the program with great enthusiasm, and before I knew it the big day came. As with every other activity in the Air Force, I would be evaluated and compared to everyone else for each jump that I made, and if I performed badly enough they would wash me out of the program. Having never jumped out of an airplane before, I had no idea what to expect. Needless to say, I was pretty scared. When it was my turn, the jump commander ordered me to the door, and when he said, "Jump," I jumped.

My exit from the airplane was less than picturesque. I was supposed to leave the aircraft gracefully with my face and body aerodynamically directed toward the front of the airplane. Then as I fell, I was supposed to arch my back so that I would gradually fall face-first toward the earth. All along the way I was to count down to the time at which I was supposed to pull the ripcord. Well, I literally tripped out the door, summer-saulting with arms and legs flailing all over the place. I didn't even bother to count. I just arched my back as hard as I could and pulled the ripcord. As you can probably imagine, I didn't get a very good score on that jump. I was forced to retrain on aircraft exit techniques and they told me, "One more like that and you'll be a washout." Funny thing, though: that was not my worst jump!

My second jump went well enough, except for the fact that this time I knew what to expect and was scared out of my gourd. But it was my third jump that was the real doozy. It was late in the afternoon and the wind was starting to pick up. According to the safety guidelines we were not allowed to jump in winds that exceeded 15 knots. When the aircraft took off everything was fine. I was psyched for a perfect jump. At altitude the jump commander ordered me to the door. I jumped and everything went perfectly. As my parachute opened, though, I noticed that no one jumped out after me. I was just a little confused because I was the second of sixteen in the jump order. There should have been at least 14 other guys jumping out after me.

"Oh well," I thought. "I'd better focus on executing a perfect PLF (parachute landing fall)." I drifted along for a few minutes when I noticed that I wasn't descending and that I was moving pretty fast. Then I realized what was going on. The wind had picked up significantly and I was being "blown about by every wind of doctrine." Eventually I did make it to the ground, but my landing was not a pretty sight. By this time I was at least one mile away from the drop zone and the wind was blowing at approximately 20 knots. Now, what you need to know is that the type of parachute we were using has a forward air speed of approximately 10 knots. So, I was traveling 10 knots forward into a 20-knot headwind. Essentially, I hit the ground going backwards at about 12 miles per hour. My wheelchair doesn't even go that fast. When I hit the ground my perfect PLF looked like a human slinky. My feet hit, then my backside, then my head. I think that my head was the focal point of impact.

When I came to, I realized that the wind was still causing me a great deal of havoc. In other words, my parachute was still inflated, dragging me across the desert floor. But this time my training served me well. I rolled to my right, grabbed the pin on my left shoulder to release the parachute cords, and subsequently halted my imitation of a bulldozer. Unfortunately, my troubles were not over yet. As I rolled to my right, a friendly neighborhood cactus plant reached out and grabbed my emergency parachute ripcord and deployed it all over the desert floor, along with my main chute and me. It was at this time that one more problem became very painfully obvious. Not only did that friendly neighborhood cactus plant grab my emergency ripcord, but it also grabbed me—in the shoulder and right in the "you know where." I looked like Wyle E. Coyote after chasing Roadrunner through a cactus patch. I had 3-inch cactus quills sticking right through my jump suit, and boy did they hurt.

I very dejectedly prepared to make the long hike back to the command post. I gathered up both chutes into a duffel bag weighing approximately 50 pounds, threw it over my left shoulder (for obvious reasons) and walked back, fully expecting to be washed out of the program. As I approached the evaluator's table, he reached out and grabbed my hand, shook it, and said, "Congratulations, You scored a perfect jump!" I found out later that the only reason I got a perfect score was because I was so far from the drop zone that they couldn't see my landing. But I wasn't about to argue with them. The guy who jumped out before me got a perfect score too, even though he was blown farther from the drop zone and landed in a clump of pine trees.

Well, to make a long story short, I jumped two more times and earned my "Jump Wings," thus ending my illustrious career as an Air Force parachute expert. For me that was an opportunity of a lifetime. Had it not been forced upon me, I probably would never have done it. But now I am glad that I did—not only for the thrill of the experience, but also because it taught me a lesson about going on when you don't want to.

Another of those unforgettable experiences took place during the summer after my freshman year. We were in a mock POW camp. Now part of being a good soldier in the Armed Forces of the United States of America is the obligation to try to escape if the enemy ever captures you. While we were in the compound picking up rocks and putting them in piles for no reason at all, I decided that I had to try to escape. I noticed that the front gate of the compound was opened just enough for me to squeeze through. I knew that there was a perimeter guard, and even though they had taken the shoelaces out of my boots, I figured that I could sneak into the woods before I was noticed. I casually walked by the guard tower and toward the gate, picking up rocks along the way. As I got to the gate everything seemed to be going great. Nobody had noticed me yet.

All of the sudden, there was a great deal of screaming and shouting from the guard tower. I thought I had been spotted, so I took off as fast as I could toward the woods. Just then, the perimeter guard came around the corner of the compound and saw me making a break for it. She tried to intercept me just before I got to the woods, but by this time I was fully committed to this intended course of action. I looked like Refrigerator Perry crashing through the front line on a goal line stand. I dipped my shoulder, plowed her over, and disappeared into the trees.

Whenever anyone escaped, they were to go to a designated place, pick up a token to prove that they had made it there, and then return to the compound in a designated period of time. The reward for escaping was an hour of sleep and a meal, which I was looking forward to with a great deal of anticipation. As I came walking back into the compound, I was rudely informed that my escape was unsuccessful. I had been shot and killed. No sleep, no meal, no nothing! What a bummer! They escorted me right back into the compound and took me to the reactionary, the place where we were punished if we were bad prisoners (or "criminals" as the guards affectionately liked to call us). I can remember thinking how unfair that was. I had escaped, was shot and killed, and now I was being punished for it. I thought I was supposed to be dead. But, nothing in a POW camp is fair.

That was a valuable lesson to learn, for many things in this life are unfair. After the training was over and we were debriefed, a few interesting facts came to light. First, all the commotion from the guard tower was because they had spotted a grizzly bear just outside the perimeter of the camp. Fortunately for me, he went one way and I went the other. Second, they told me that they had never before seen anyone run so fast without shoelaces in their boots. And third, they told me that it was probably the best escape attempt they had seen because of its simplicity. Oh well, too bad it didn't work.

The Academy days were fun and challenging. They were a blessing in many ways, yet in the midst of God's abundant blessing, I had more very important lessons to learn—lessons that were going to try my faith deeply and stretch me beyond what I could ever imagine possible. God had a grand plan for my life; I just didn't know what it was yet.

Jim was our second son to go to the Air Force Academy. John had graduated from there in 1975. How proud we were of our Air Force Cadets! The first parent's weekend I thought my husband would never be able to button his shirtfront again. His chest fairly burst with pride. God did indeed bless us. Doug's cancer had been removed and he was strong and healthy again. Our children were all doing well. They had all come to know the Lord except for John, the oldest. Prayer would take care of that we were sure. Everything was going so well.

A New Challenge

It was October 29, 1980, a day just like any other. I was a sophomore at the United States Air Force Academy and life was pretty routine. I had gone to classes and was supposed to spend the rest of the afternoon at track practice, but that day there was going to be a special air show at Pete Field, the local airfield. We were anticipating the possibility of being able to see up close an F-15, A-10, and an SR-71. Since it was my dream to fly fighters, I wanted to go to the air show. So, I asked my coach if it would be all right to skip track practice. I was granted permission and immediately went up to my squadron and caught a ride with an upper classman, Marty Waugh, and my roommate, Richard Fullerton. I was sitting in the back seat. We were traveling east out of town when we were broadsided by a van. No one was hurt but me. I was lying in the back seat completely unable to move. My fifth and sixth cervical vertebrae had separated, and I was instantly and completely paralyzed from the shoulders down. All of my other injuries were minor, consisting of some bruises and cuts from flying glass. It's funny how separating two very small bones can result in so much devastation to the body. But that's all that happened. The accident wasn't even that serious, but it changed my life forever. I really have no recollection of the events that immediately followed, but I do know that I was in critical condition and it was questionable if I would even live.

No one can imagine the impact of the telephone call that came that night unless they themselves have lived through it. Not only did the accident change Jim's life forever, but it changed the lives of so many others, primarily his family. That phone call came in the evening while I was baby sitting my new and first grandson. I was alone because Doug had gone to the Wednesday night prayer service at church and son, JD, had taken my step-grandson out to entertain him for a bit. John and his wife would be returning that night from a short trip.

The impersonal, yet not unsympathetic, voice of the neurosurgeon told of Jim's injury as being irreparable. Jim was paralyzed from the neck down. He would never move his lower body by himself again. He would never move his limbs, sit, stand or walk by himself again. He spoke in terms that I could understand and yet I did not. I kept asking what could be done. What was being done? He continued to tell me there was absolutely no hope. This injury was not curable and there was no chance of reversal. The vertebrae had been injured and paralysis was complete from that point to the rest of Jim's body for the rest of his life. I didn't believe him. I refused to believe this was true. All I could think of was that my child was hurt and I must get to him as soon as possible. I felt that I must get Doug and we must get on a plane instantly and get to Jim. There was no reasoning. I just had to get to my child and hold him tight because he was hurt.

I called the church and asked for them to send Doug home. They wanted me to come there for prayer, but that was beyond me at that point. I couldn't seem to function past calling the airport to get seats to Colorado Springs. Several people from the church came home with Doug to pray; but home by then was chaos. I was crying uncontrollably and my oldest son had come home to find his baby crying, his step-son crying, his mother crying, his brother trying valiantly to be a man *and calm everyone down, people in the house praying aloud, and his father shouting and shaking his fist at God. What a picture that calls to mind years later. However, then it seemed a house so full of despair it was impossible to describe.*

We finally got plane tickets arranged for the next morning. A dear couple from our church, the Goulds, arrived at our door that evening with two more airline tickets for JD and Kim. It was a great comfort to know they would both be with us. We also calmed down enough to make some inquiries about spinal cord injuries and spent the night calling to get information about what could be done, if anything, to minimize the injury. We prayed all the way out to Colorado and I was certain God was listening. Only He could change things, but He would do it.

We arrived in C Springs the next day and found Jim in a semi-comatose state. Whether he knew we had arrived or not, I don't know. We were there with him. I couldn't hold him in my arms, but I could touch him and assure him of my love.

The next two weeks were critical. The greatest challenge that I had ever faced now involved life and death. Before I was out of intensive care, I came close to dying three times.

The first time was immediately after the accident when my body went into spinal shock (basically, that means that my central nervous system shut down). My brain was no longer connected to the rest of my body (although, some might argue that it never was)! Everything felt numb, as if my body was injected with novocaine. I could see my legs, but couldn't feel a thing. Even now, I am unable to feel anything from my shoulders down. I can imagine where my arms and legs are, but unless I can see them I really have no idea. When I tell children that I can't feel anything, they like to ask, "what if" questions. "What if I pinched your leg? Could you feel it?" I tell them, "You could even chop off my finger and I wouldn't know it unless I saw it with my eyes!"

Before anything else could begin to happen, I had to be stabilized.. This involved tubes and monitors and machines and all kinds of stuff. They stretched me out on a special bed called a Stryker frame. Then they strapped my feet securely to one end, screwed metal pins into my skull just above each ear, strung small cables from the pins over a pulley system at the top of my bed and hung 35 pounds of weight off the other end. What a headache! It's called traction, but I think that it dates back to some of the medieval torture devices used during the Inquisition. The Stryker frame (also known affectionately as the "sandwich bed") was an ingenious contraption. When I could no longer tolerate lying on my back, they would put a framed piece of canvas on top of me, secure it to the piece that was under me, and rotate it 180 degrees to the left or to the right, so that I was then face down. Then they would leave me in that position, which, by the way, was less tolerable than before. I can remember my coaches, buddies, and officers from the Academy visiting me and crawling under me to lie face up on the floor so that they could talk with me as I was lying face down in the bed. That's how my parents first saw me. I can't imagine how difficult that must have been for them. It wasn't long after this that they decided to put me in a variation of the Stryker frame called a circle bed. Instead of flipping me from side to side like a hamburger on the grill, this bed flipped me head over toe like a spring-

36

board diver. I'm not sure why they put me in this kind of bed, but it was no more pleasant than the first.

The whole family came to Colorado Springs. John came from California where he was stationed with the Air Force. Jackie also came from California where she was visiting a friend. JD came on the plane with Doug and me.

God made His presence felt the minute we arrived at the airport. Jim's officers were there to meet us and take us to the hospital. At the hospital there were people from the Baptist Student Union where Jim had been an active member. They arranged for us to stay at the Student Union where we would have a great degree of privacy. They also came up with a loaner car to use while in Colorado Springs. People brought us food, linens, and compassion. Someone was available all the time.

The churches of the area sent their representatives and assured us of their continuing prayers. The students sent cards and letters, some of which were so touching. One boy sent a letter to Jim of 22 pages, line after line of which read: "You will walk again." "You will walk again." The encouragement of those positive lines was so needed because it was so hard to see Jim lying like the filling of a sandwich in that horrible contrivance.

Almost worse than the sandwich-flipping contraption was the metal halo attached to his head and neck by big old bolts driven right into his skull. They weren't tiny little surgical drill holes; they were quarter inch bolts! He was absolutely immobile except for his mouth and eyes. Seeing him that way was almost more than we could take. We would put on. a brave front while in the hospital; and then go back to our quarters and just hold each other and cry and cry.

Jim's Path

Jim stayed in Colorado Springs in intensive care about five days. When the doctors considered him stabilized (no longer in danger of immediate death) he was flown to Fitzsimmons Army Hospital in Denver. There we were to know without doubt that God was with us all the way.

My second bout with death also came as a result of spinal shock. I started to have difficulty breathing on my own. It was determined that I would have to have a tracheotomy and be connected to a ventilator in order to breathe sufficiently. This was another medieval torture device designed to make you gasp in panic for air. Actually, the decision to go ahead with a tracheotomy resulted in two blessings. First, I was able to breathe again, a must if you are going to continue to live. And second, as they were administering some muscle relaxants around my neck to do the procedure, the two vertebrae that were separated snapped back into place. The doctors determined that they should do a spinal fusion immediately. This involves fusing the two broken vertebrae together into one in order to stabilize the spinal column. After those two operations, it was back into the circle bed for me.

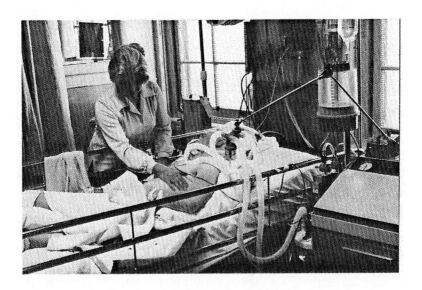

One night, as I was lying face down in torture device #1, the circle bed, my head fell through the small hole that exposed my face and enough of my neck to connect the ventilator. I couldn't lift my head up because my neck was broken. The tube from my ventilator was pinched off by the weight of my head. I couldn't breathe at all. Just then, as the alarm sounded, a nurse was walking by. She gently lifted my head back into place as I was gasping for air. My second bout with death was over and God had sovereignly allowed me to continue living. Well, fortunately for me, that was it for the circle bed. They put me on the real bed with a neck brace and rolled me from side to side every two hours to prevent pressure sores.

Fortunately for us, we were not aware of Jim's near brush with death on that occasion. We were given rooms in the Officer's Quarters on the hospital grounds. These were barracks type rooms, very spartan and uncomfortable; but we were grateful for a place to stay so close to the hospital because we spent every moment there except for sleeping.

Our day began as we entered the hospital and faced the chapel door. It was a beautiful little chapel with a big marble archway over the door. On the marble was engraved Psalm 46:10, "Be Still and Know that I Am God." Those words blessed me every day for the six weeks that I was to remain there. I know they blessed Doug and the rest of the family, too. We were reminded of who was in charge every morning at the very beginning of the day.

Most of the time during that six weeks I was alone. John had to get back to his family and his duties, Jackie and JD had to go back to school and Doug had to get back to Medina to work and to continue treatments for any stray cancer cells that might have escaped. Because I was alone, it was even more comforting to see those words and know that Christ was with me. I had a comforter who would control everything for me.

I still struggled with the "Why not someone else?" question. Christ wanted me to learn about others' problems. When I saw a woman sobbing in the waiting area, I felt so sorry for her. However, when she told me that her husband was to lose an arm because of injury; I thought to myself, "An arm!" Only an arm? How hard would it be to adjust to the loss of an arm as compared to the loss of all body function?" What was she crying about? She still had a husband with one arm to hold her and he could still touch his children and feel their soft little fingers in his remaining hand. He could learn to care for himself. He could feel and he could walk tall. Compared to my son, he was lucky! Still, a small quiet voice told me that I *should care for her and sympathize too. I tried. I offered to share my little room with her because she had no place to stay near the hospital. She stayed a few days while I valiantly tried to hold in my resentment. The Lord really needed to work on me.*

My third bout with death also came as a result of spinal shock. As you can see, spinal shock is a real bummer. I started to bleed internally. The doctors had a suspicion that it was caused by a duodenal ulcer. Gastric juices were pouring into my stomach and my brain wasn't getting the message to turn them off. These juices had literally eaten a hole in a major artery in my stomach. This is a typical problem with spinal cord injuries. In order to verify that this was the problem, they did an esophageal duodenoscopy. They stuck a small tube (it felt like it was about the size of a garden hose) down my throat to look at my stomach! Major gag (the epitome of "gag me with a spoon")! This is the third of the medieval torture devices that are still in use today. I had about 15 doctors and nurses standing around my bed, viewing my ulcer. When the doctor in charge asked if anyone else wanted to see it, I motioned as best I could to him that I did (a major accomplishment for a guy who is paralyzed and has a hose-sized tube stuck down his throat). He held the scope to my eye and I got to see my own ulcer.

That could have been the last thing I ever saw. I was bleeding so badly that my eyes rolled back into my head and my heart stopped. There was no more blood in my body to pump. Fortunately, there was plenty of help immediately available. They got my heart started again and began filling me back up with blood. My fuel gauge was so low that they ran out of blood and had to sequester help to get more from the blood bank. My younger brother, J.D., was sitting in the waiting room when he heard the call for help. He immediately dashed down three flights of stairs to the blood bank and carried back up as much as he could. When my tank was full, they wheeled me off for emergency surgery on my stomach. The doctor, who was a believer, said that when he opened me up, he literally had to reach into my stomach and pinch off the bleeder with his finger and thumb, otherwise I would have died on the operating table. But God had a plan and He wasn't through with me yet.

God surely was in control here. Each morning as we would come into the hospital, there was that chapel door with its poignant message. We would go in to pray and there, kneeling in the front pew, was always the same man. He was always there at the same time and he was always on his knees. Imagine our encouragement and confidence in the outcome of this crucial surgery when we saw the man who was to perform it! Our morning kneeler turned out to be the head of surgery in the spinal cord department and a man who really loved the Lord. He went to the Lord daily to ask His guidance before he started surgery. He was to do the necessary surgery for Jim. Praise God for the comfort that gave us!

Waiting for the outcome of perilous surgery is a time of intense emotion. You think you can't get through it. Your heart leaps at every movement and your mind whirls around like a squirrel cage. I was no exception to these feelings. I was clearly in great distress. God came to my rescue again when he placed a young lady by my side. I have no idea who she was or why she was there. I like to believe that she was an angel just sent for me. She comforted me and sat holding my hand. She brought

*me food and drink. Most important, she gave me a small book
that gave me immense hope and comfort for the immediate
future and also for many years to come. I still keep it close. It
was the "Pocket Book of Jesus' Promises". What wonderful
promises they are. I could look at those and then 'Be still and
know that He is God.' He would take care of it all.*

Let me just add two neat side notes here. First, in response to my need for so much blood, almost all of the 4000
cadets at the Academy donated blood to the blood bank.
Second, the doctor who performed my surgery was no
stranger to my parents. Every morning before visiting hours,
Mom and Dad would go to the hospital Chapel to pray, and
every morning they noticed an older gentleman on his knees
in the front of the Chapel praying also. Psalm 46:10, "Be
still and know that I am God," etched across the front of
the room, was a great comfort to my parents. When they
found out that I needed to have major stomach surgery,
they were introduced to the surgeon who would perform
the operation. Much to their surprise and relief, the surgeon was the elderly gentleman from the Chapel. He prayed
every morning that God would guide his hands as he performed his daily surgeries. Indeed God did have a special
plan for my life, and He was using His servants from all
walks of life to minister to my needs.

I can't count the times that people told me that God
must have a special plan for my life because He allowed me
to live through all of that. I didn't like those words. I didn't
like what God was doing in my life. I liked my life the way
it was before. If this was His plan, I didn't want anything to
do with it. There were times I wished that God hadn't even
allowed me to live; and if I could have, I would have ended

it all. But I was so helpless, I couldn't even do that. Praise God I couldn't! For God is good, and His plan is perfect! Yet, I still had many lessons to learn before I would willingly submit myself to His will.

Facing Reality

At first, facing the reality of what had happened to me was very difficult. In fact, I denied it. I can remember thinking to myself after spending two weeks in the hospital that I had to get back to school. I was already so far behind that it would take a miracle just to get caught up. And, what about track practice? I had to get back to practice. The indoor season was starting soon, and I had to get ready. These thoughts went through my head as I lay there paralyzed from the shoulders down. Then the reality of my circumstances crashed in on me in a brutal way. One day as I was lying in bed, a physical therapist was ranging out my legs (that's just a fancy medical way of saying that he was stretching my legs). It was the first time after my accident that I was able to see my legs, because the brace on my neck restricted my ability to look down at my body. I can remember vividly him lifting my left leg into a position where I could see it. It was nothing but skin and bone, bulging at the knee like the pictures you see on TV of starving people in Africa. I couldn't believe my eyes. I was shocked. In a matter of weeks, I had gone from a six-foot, 180 pound, lean-mean pole-vaulting machine to a six-foot, 120-pound bag of bones. I felt nauseated. I closed my eyes and wished to God that I could just die. I can remember thinking to

myself that it wasn't worth it. I couldn't do this. I knew that
I couldn't live the rest of my life like this, and I wanted to
die. It would be so much easier to just go home to heaven
and be with the Lord. Reality was starting to sink in and I
didn't like it.

*Reality—what do we, the loved ones of the patient, do
when faced with it? We watched our son go from the fine physical specimen that the Academy required from their cadets to
this 129-pound length of flaccid skin and bones. He was so
helpless. He couldn't even talk because of the tracheotomy.
The only way he could communicate with us was by clicking
his tongue. 'No' was one click,' yes' was two clicks. How we
hurt to see him suffer so. Not only did we see Jim suffer, but we
were surrounded by suffering. A spinal cord injury unit is an
ICU for everyone in it. Everyone there is on the edge of death.
Yet we saw love there that you would never witness in better
circumstances. A wife came with her children each day to
hug and hold their father. An elderly wife came to try to get
her long time spouse to eat just one spoonful of Jell-O. With
her eyes full of tears she would urge him to try to live for her.
One woman came every day to sit by her son who was coma-
tose. He had been that way for six weeks. She still came faithfully each day and stayed all day holding his hand and talking
to his unresponsive body. What a wonderful picture of our Lord
Jesus Christ, who faithfully attends our needs and calls to us
even when we are unresponsive. Never do you see such sacrificial love out in the everyday world. Life in the spinal cord
injury unit was heart-rending; but, oh, so beautiful, too.*

*How do we face reality there? One day at a time, we
encourage each other, draw closer than brothers and sisters,*

hug and agonize over the little advances or setbacks, and trust the Lord to help us each day.

It was right about this time when life gave me another cold slap in the face. One day as I was lying in bed paralyzed from the shoulders down, I received a visitor. She was a total stranger, but said that she came to encourage me in the Lord. She then proceeded to tell me that if I would confess all of my sins, God would heal me. She said it was because I was harboring sin in my heart that God was dealing so harshly with me. If I were right with God, I wouldn't be in this condition. Needless to say, that didn't go over very well. I knew I wasn't harboring sin in my heart. I knew there were no unconfessed sins. And I knew that I was trying my best to trust in God and wait on Him. She made me feel like there must be some deep, hidden sin in my life that I had to confess in order to get right with God. I felt like making some up, just to make sure that I had covered all the bases. What a distorted view of the kind and gracious God we serve!

That lady's attempt to encourage me did just the opposite. I was deflated, uncertain, and demoralized. I praise God that He had already surrounded me with a number of people who offered me good, godly, sound, biblical council, which encouraged me a great deal in the days to follow. Since then, I have run into a number of people just like her. I've had total strangers lay hands on me and pray for healing. I've had people give me good luck charms that were supposed to bring healing. I've had people invite me to healing services. These people offer miracles that they cannot guarantee. They offer hope that is biblically unfounded. They offer encouragement that ultimately results in multiplied discouragement.

We met a number of people just like the woman Jim described; but they were few in comparison to the number of Christian people God sent to keep us from total despair. Pastor Magnus was one. He came from a church near Denver, up in the mountains somewhere. He came every day to give encouragement and love. There were others from the churches in the area and from Colorado Springs. Mary and Paul, I know them only by those names, were familiar with the spinal cord injury unit. Paul had been a patient there. He was better now; but came back every day to encourage others to fight for life. He had Christ in his heart. So did Mary. Many of Jim's friends from the Academy and the Baptist Student Union came to encourage. Often total strangers came to offer their friendship and love. One such woman had the last name of Bright. She was as bright as her name. I had been at Fitzsimmons for nearly six weeks, most often by myself because JD and Jackie had to get back to school and Doug had to be getting his cancer treatments back home in Medina. I was very depressed and lonely when Gracie's brightness shone on me. She came in like a ray of sunshine and introduced herself by saying, "You need to get out of this hospital and I'm taking you for an hour or so." She took me to a mall for lunch and to sit in a sun puddle in the mall where I could watch the people walk back and forth. It was so wonderful just to see a normal world again and to realize it still existed.

There were so many more of God's servants. I wish I could tell you of them all.

After six weeks in ICU at Fitzsimmons Hospital, it was determined that Jim was well enough to begin rehabilitation.

He still had major strides to make. First he had to get off the respirator and breathe on his own. Then he had to learn to sit up again and get his heart to pump the blood vertically instead of horizontally as it had been doing for seven weeks. Then would come the real rehab—learning to live in a wheelchair. To do this he would be airlifted to a large Medical Center for military veterans in the Midwest. The center was considered to be the best hospital for rehabilitation nearest to our home in Ohio.

Jim was put on a medical plane and I was allowed to fly with him. Can you believe this hardy parachuter of only a few weeks ago was now petrified of flying? He was very frightened of being moved at all.

The military was considerate of all his needs. He had his own special nurse to fly with him and assure him that the respirator on which he depended for his every breath would continue to provide him with the necessary oxygen all the way. She was extremely compassionate and efficient. It was in this manner that a new phase of our long journey back to life began.

It was at this midwestern veteran's hospital that the monster respirator was conquered.

As I look back now, I can see that God was gracious in allowing me gradually to deal with the reality of living the rest of my life in a wheelchair. I had a lot of things to deal with before I would ever face sitting in my first wheelchair. The immediate challenge was getting off the respirator.

The Battle Begins

It took me six weeks after my accident to get out of the Intensive Care Unit at the Army Hospital in Denver, Colorado. During that time God provided in many ways. Many folks from churches all over the area came to encourage my family and me. My parents were befriended and comforted by people who were total strangers but were willing to be used by God to comfort us. Just a couple of weeks before Christmas of 1980, it was determined that I should be moved to a VA in the Midwest. It was supposed to be among the best in Spinal Cord Rehabilitation. I was airlifted to Wisconsin, and placed in a 12-man ward. That would be my home for the next three months.

I believe I have already indicated that the respirator is an ingenious torture device developed during the Inquisition. It's ingenious because it confronts its victim in two ways. First, there is the suctioning. Because the trache is a foreign object in your windpipe, your body naturally secretes phlegm around it. The phlegm clogs the trach and makes it very difficult to breathe, so they suction out the phlegm. They do this by inserting a little suctioning tube into the trache and down your throat to suck out all the fluid. That doesn't sound so bad except for the fact that it causes you to gag and cough at the same time. But, you can't cough because you have no muscles to cough with. Add to that the fact that they disconnect the respirator, so you can't breathe anyhow. It's a wonderful experience that has to be endured quite often to keep your airway clear!

Then there's the second challenge. To help wean you off the respirator, they adjust how much the respirator breathes for you. The idea is to force you to breathe more and more on your own. It's a great idea, but boy, is it tough. There is no worse sensation than feeling like you can't breathe. I can remember hyperventilating often because I felt I wasn't getting enough air. As I grew stronger and stronger, they started turning the ventilator off. That was scary too! First I would go for five minutes, then 10, then eventually 30 minutes, then an hour. There were also many setbacks, times when I couldn't continue breathing on my own. I felt so discouraged I wondered if I would ever be able to breathe on my own again.

Being on the respirator was also discouraging because I couldn't talk. The trach bypassed my vocal cords. I had to try to mouth my words to whoever was listening. Mom did pretty well, but Dad was completely frustrated because he couldn't understand a thing I was trying to say. Eventually, we worked out a system of clicks that enabled me to talk on the phone. One click was "no" and two was "yes." Obviously, my conversations on the phone were short and to the point, but it did save on the long distance charges.

Phone calls were hard to get through. They did not have phones in the wards. The only phone was on a portable unit that could be wheeled from bed to bed. You had to wait your turn to get to it. However, we usually could get it once every evening. The folks at home would congregate at the Workman's who, miracle of miracles, had one of those newfangled things called an 800 number. People from the church, the Imigs and the Workmans would call and we could talk an unlimited time for free. Jim could click away to his heart's content and people quickly learned how to communicate by asking the questions that he could answer. They told him of their prayers for him.

One particularly treasured prayer was that of the Workman's little five year old. She prayed every day mightily and faithfully for Jim's healing. Such a little girl to ask so faithfully for someone else's welfare, I'm sure the Lord heard her and wept.

After struggling for six weeks to get off the respirator, I had a particularly bad setback. I had built up my stamina to the point where I could breathe on my own for an hour. Then one night, I only lasted 10 minutes before they had me back on the respirator. I was heartsick! I couldn't believe that I was going backwards again. I had to get past the respirator before I could go any further in my rehabilitation. Then, the next morning they took me off the respirator and it was over. I never needed it again. That was a significant victory. I had been freed from the shackles of a tiny little machine that literally controlled my life. Those were very difficult and discouraging days, but God was faithful and continued to work on my behalf, even in spite of me.

God was certainly not through with providing for us. He did so with more than we could hope for, both financially and with physical comfort.

The family came to Wisconsin by car from Ohio. They met me at the hospital and we met with counselors while Jim was being admitted and settled in. We were told that it was in the best interests of each patient that he leave the hospital on weekends as soon as he was able. Looking forward to a normal weekend and being away from the hospital environment was vital to the rehab process and the patient's psychological well being. Jim was not ready to leave just yet, but they assured us that they wanted to get him off the respirator and up in a wheelchair as soon as they could. They estimated about one week's time. This was very encouraging, but also put pressure on us for a place to stay. We came to Milwaukee with nothing but a few clothes in our bags. Now we had to plan for a place to stay so we could be near Jim for several months. To add to the pressure, Christmas was coming in just a couple of weeks. We desperately wanted the family to be together at Christmas time.

We had settled into a motel suite that consisted of just one large room with a kitchenette/dinette at one end. To cram five people, one of whom was in a wheelchair, into that space was not very reasonable. In addition, it was quite expensive to stay in a motel for six or seven months. Therefore, whenever we had free time we began looking for an apartment that would be accessible for handicapped people. We looked and looked to no avail. Everything had steps, the bathroom doors were too narrow, or the hall turned too sharply for Jim to negotiate. Finally, on the first Saturday after our arrival, we found an apartment! It was just across the street from the VA hospital, too! God does answer prayer, as we have need. The apartment smelled like smoke; it was cramped and ugly with dingy furniture; it was furnished, but only with a few pieces, there were no linens, dishes, cooking utensils, or homey amenities; but, hey, it was a place where we could all be together. We could drag all that stuff from Ohio and make it home. Thanking the Lord, we told the landlord that we would take it. He said, "Fine, I'll need $500 cash to hold it for you." We didn't carry $500 in cash with us. It was after 3 o'clock on a Saturday afternoon and all the banks were closed. In 1980 there were no ATM's and the landlord wouldn't accept a personal check.

"God, You should have worked this out a little better!"

We left praying that He would see that the apartment was still there for us on Monday. Little did we suspect that, as usual, God had something far better in mind for us.

The next day, Sunday, while we were with Jim, a lady came to us asking to talk. We sat down with her and she explained her proposition. Her parents had gone to Arizona for the winter and had rented their home to a family who were to be relocated in Wisconsin. The father's transfer had been changed and they had to renege on the rental of the home. This lovely lady wanted to know if we would be interested in renting the home in their stead. She had heard about us and our need through her church and had come all the way down to the hospital to offer the house to us. What a perfect gift to us! The house was a beautiful home in a very nice neighborhood. It was easily accessible with only one small step into the entire first floor. It was a large house with two bedrooms on the ground floor and three up; so Jim could be accommodated as well as the rest of the family. It was beautifully and comfortably furnished with every need we might have, even to a box of Christmas tree ornaments in the basement. In addition, it was much cheaper than the apartment we had been so anxious about. Gods gifts are always more perfect than our little minds can conceive of.

During this time, money, or lack of it, was a constant concern. We had been using up our rainy day savings at a rapid pace. Now we were contemplating renting a second home, flying or driving back and forth between Wisconsin and Medina, Ohio, and incurring other expenses along the way.

Other demoralizing news had come our way. Doug's cancer had reappeared in his lungs. The doctor's prognosis was not encouraging but they were willing to try some experimen-

tal drugs in hopes that would help. Somehow we had to stay near Jim; but Doug had to be near to his cancer treatments, too, so he could get chemotherapy on a weekly basis. JD and Jackie would often drive the seven hours to Wisconsin, but that was getting to be too much of a strain for Doug. He insisted on being near us and if he hadn't, I don't know what I would have done. I needed to be with Jim and I needed to be with my husband who was suffering too. The days had to be gotten through one at a time.

Day by day, God saw to our needs. The cards and letters poured in from our friends and all the church members. More often than not, they contained checks or money orders for our use. Also, the high school where I taught, and which the children had all attended, put on a benefit show. All the children had been very active in the school choir performances and so the choir performed and the community responded. The proceeds were a greatly needed blessing.

My colleagues were a blessing, too. My sick days had run out and I no longer was getting a paycheck, so our income was diminished. All the teachers on the faculty offered to donate one of their sick days to me. That would have been 100 days or about five months of salary. Although the State of Ohio would not allow the transfer of sick days, the offer really warmed my heart.

Jim was in a private room for the first few days at the VA. He had first to get off that respirator. What a battle that was for him! He had a very patient doctor who encouraged him at every setback. He was one of the few employees at the VA whom we really admired. I include in the term employees: nurses, doctors, therapists, aides, and psychologists. Another doctor whom we really liked was an Indian woman whose *command of the English language was a bit shaky. She would come in every morning and check Jim's lung capacity. When discussing the volume of air he was getting into his lungs she would say, "Oh! Your walloms are good today." We looked forward to hearing about Jim's 'walloms' because that meant his breathing was progressing.*

One day, Jim's right leg was hugely swollen. He had a thrombosis in that leg. It was a great worry for several days. Then one morning she came in to check him out, looked under the covers, and said, "Your leg is gone!" We would have been appalled to hear that, except she said it with such a cheery voice. Indeed, Jim's leg was not gone. She only meant to say that the swelling was gone. Jim still had his leg, thanks be to God.

While Jim battled the respirator, we adjusted to the spinal cord unit at the Wisconsin VA. Since he was not yet in a ward, we met others who were in private rooms. This was fortunate for us, since it gave us a little time to get used to his and to our being there. The VA hospital was not a cheery place. It seemed that most of the patients had no family to care about them. They were lonely and mostly in despair. This affected all those around them, especially their primary caretakers. The nurses had a very hard time not allowing the patients depression to affect them.

My heart still bleeds for one man next to Jim. He was far from home and had no visitors. He had a wife and family but they could not afford to leave their home to be with him. He had fallen down some stairs in his home and suffered a very high injury which meant that he had hardly any function below his face. He could eat, drink, and cry. He did very little of the first two and a lot of the latter. He could not get off the respirator so he couldn't talk to us. We could only go in often and hold his hand while the tears rolled and rolled and rolled down his cheeks.

Dark Days

We tried to make my little corner of that 12-man ward as comfortable as possible. There wasn't much privacy, but there was a lot of smoke. It seemed like every other patient in the room smoked at least two cartons a day. For a guy who had never smoked and who was trying to build up his lung capacity after being weaned off a respirator, it made life pretty miserable. I had my own TV, three drawers (the top one was always filled with M&Ms, my favorite candies), and a small closet. I had a window next to my bed. The walls were painted institutional green. It wasn't very homey, but we did the best we could by hanging encouraging cards and posters on the wall, and balloons around my bed.

Jim's description of the ward in the VA really needs enhancing to give the real picture. We did our best to brighten up his little corner. There was little we could do to dispel the smoke. We could pull the curtains but that didn't help much and seemed to shut us away from the other men and to give the impression that we thought we were too good for the others. Therefore, we suffered the thick smoke. Jim was not exaggerating when he said it was awful. Every man on the ward smoked heavily. Jim was the only non-smoker. Those who were paralyzed from the shoulders down (most of them) could not lift the cigarette up to their mouths so the nurses rigged up an apparatus from which they could puff constantly. They would position a tube attached to the cigarette on the wheelchair arm or bed railing. The tube reached to their mouths and they could puff their lives away.

The VA's attitude seemed to be "You can't do any thing about your misfortune, so do everything you can to forget it." Alcohol was a big antidote to the men's depression and one that the hospital condoned. Once or twice a week the nurses would get the men all positioned in their chairs and make a grand exodus to the bar across the street from the hospital. There the men could drink all they wanted, taking hospital volunteers along to hold their glasses for them.

Getting used to seeing men who lived their lives lying on a wheeled bed on their stomachs, who sat slumped in a chair puffing on a nicotine tube, or who simply lay and stared at the ceiling, took a lot of stamina. Realizing that our son was no longer that snappy Air Force Cadet; but one of those helpless men, took us to the depths of humility. God really dealt our pride a series of big blows. How much it hurt to see my beautiful son in such a helpless condition is indescribable. I remember watching the little receptionist at the desk as she disdainfully directed the men who were so hurt. I was so angry! Didn't she know that <u>my son</u> was one of the most eligible men in the universe? He was worth ten of her type! Jesus really had a hard task when he began to humble me!

Sometimes my anger was fair and honest though. Jim told me about asking a nurse to help him, when he had fallen over in his chair and couldn't right himself. She had replied that she was on her coffee break, which meant that he would have to stay hanging over the arm of the chair, head down, until time for her to go back to work. That day my anger was righteous anger.

My description of the spinal cord injury ward has so far been only of the down side. There was definitely an up side where one couldn't deny the Lord at work through his people. They literally thronged to Jim's bedside.

The first to arrive was Carl and later his wife, Jeanne, and their two boys. Carl was the liaison officer for the Air Force and he did his job far beyond what was required of him. His was a very active family in the city, in business, community and the church. However, from the time Jim arrived at the VA, it seemed that they put their lives on hold and lived just for the Fritzes. They came to the hospital to spend time with all of us. Their two boys brought their guitars and played and sang. When they heard that it was better therapeutically for Jim to come home every weekend, it was Carl, Jeanne and the boys who came to help get Jim into the car and then into the house both going and coming. Doug was no longer strong enough to do it and neither was I.

They were there for pizza parties. They were there for encouragement and prayer. Best of all, I never went to bed at night without Jeanne's phone call to see if I had arrived home safely and was alright for the night.

Then there was Gus. He came every day to pray with Jim and to bring him a milk shake. He was determined to build up this boy of mine. What a prayer warrior he was! I knew the Lord was listening to him. Gus gave so much encouragement through his prayers.

The O'Gormans were a pair of brothers who led a youth group in their church. They would come with their entire group and fill the ward with songs and laughter. They encouraged Jim to go out with them to healthy activities. They were the group that took him to the "Joni" film.

There was Ginnie. She came to see to my sanity. She took me to lunch and to her home. She got her hairdresser to come to cut Jim's hair. She did so many little things that most of us don't even think of as being necessary until we're in the hospital in a strange place.

God sent Scott, a young man from Carl and Jeanne's church. He came faithfully to play games with Jim, to talk, and just to be a friend. He was an exceptional friend, too, because most of the time Jim was depressed and not too receptive to Scott's overtures. Scott ignored Jim's rudeness and just kept on coming and talking and being there for a friend who really needed a friend.

The Eastwood boys came from Medina all the way to Wisconsin more than once. If ever there was a pair of friends who were more than brothers, it was the Eastwood boys.

Scott came from the Academy during his Christmas vacation. I can still remember the laughter as he did a "Rapture Practice." He would draw up his considerably lengthy body and then jump as high into the air as he could shouting, "Rapture Practice!" as he leaped.

All this good will and laughter and cheeriness had its effect on the rest of the ward, too. The other men would be included if they wanted to be. A lot of them did. Some looked with disdain on the Christian hope and faith, but nevertheless, I think all of them wished they could be a part of God's family as Jim was. Maybe the seeds were planted. I like to think so. One man I know felt a change of heart. He was a man of about forty with a wife and four kids. He had fallen off a ladder while working on his house and he was paralyzed from the neck down. His wife had taken his children and divorced him. He was alone in the world and had very little to live for. How-

ever, after we had all been there for about two months, he be-gan to join us and to ask a few questions. I don't know the outcome of his search. I do know he began to think out of him-self and to care about others' welfare. On Jim's 20th birthday, he pestered and pleaded with everyone he came in contact with, to go out and buy him a BIG bag of M&M's. He knew Jim's fondness for them and he provided Jim with enough M&M's to last for a long, long time. He felt so badly for Jim because he was hurt at such a very young age and his compassion was very clear in his eyes.

That was the upside of our time at that VA and those fond memories of God's gracious provision have almost obliterated the dreariness and despair we saw.

One of the first orders of business was getting me used to sitting up again. After lying in bed for six weeks, sitting up was a very dizzying experience because my heart was not used to pumping my blood against gravity anymore. Once again, I was privileged to be a participant in another torture device called THE TABLE! It was a very simple de-vice designed to make the victim pass out. They would lay me on this table, strap me down, and tilt it forward until I was in a standing position. The first time, I made it to five degrees and I was out. They did that over and over until I made it to 30 degrees. I can remember saying, as they were tilting the table, "I'm going! I'm going! I'M GOING!" Then everything went black and I was gone. It wasn't very fun, but it worked and I was up in a wheelchair in no time.

Once I was able to get into a wheelchair, I settled down into a daily routine, which consisted of getting up in the morning, going to physical therapy, eating lunch, going to occupational therapy, free time, eating dinner, and going to bed. That was more complicated than it looks, for though this particular VA was touted as a great rehabilitation center, their nursing staff was terrible. There were many days that I missed all of my therapy sessions because I was still in bed at lunchtime. Out of desperation and sheer frustration, my mom took it upon herself to learn how to get me out of bed. For the next three months, she got me up and dressed every morning, so that I would be able to make it to my therapy sessions. Eventually, the nurses got so used to her being there that they expected it, and if mom didn't come in, I didn't get up. Let me insert a personal note here. Mom, I love you! God blessed me with a wonderful mother who was willing to make tremendous sacrifices for me. I thank God for her, for I know that I would not be where I am today if it hadn't been for her sacrificial love.

I thank God for Jim! What an inspiration he has been for all of us. He is the one who has sacrificed so much, so that all of us could change to conform more to what Jesus wants us to be. What a strong Christian he has become! We have all grown in Christ and closer to Christ through Jim's trials.

Though all of this was so hard at the time, I can look back now and see how God was using it all to change us and help us focus on Him.

I had a great deal of anger at those nurses who didn't do their jobs well. Later, when Jim was transferred to another rehab facility I saw every patient up and taken to breakfast by 8 o'clock, so my anger was not misplaced. Good nursing is the result of good administration.

It was not easy for me to get to that hospital by seven in the morning. Most days Doug insisted on coming with me so I had to assist him as he was not able to do much for himself anymore. It was heartbreaking for me to see my beloved husband sit hour after hour in a straight chair, just to be near Jim and hold his hand. I knew he was in great pain, but I also knew he had to be with his son. Jim recognized his pain, too, but somehow their being together comforted both of them.

Our days started at seven when I would get Jim in the shower. I can still remember that we were the only ones who sang in the shower. We sang joyful songs at the tops of our voices. I hope it conveyed some hope, but knowing how my voice is, maybe it was just a joyful noise to the Lord.

We tried to keep everything as normal as possible. To that end, we bought the latest styles for Jim to wear. He was the only man there to take care of his appearance. The other men didn't bother to shave, comb their hair, or dress in other than a sloppy tee shirt. Some didn't even change out of the hospital pajama shirt. Probably it was too much of a hassle to get the nurses to attend to toiletries and frills like decent clothes.

We loved our Jim. He was so handsome. Just because he couldn't dress and care for himself didn't mean he had to look like no one loved him. Therefore, he was always dressed in cheerful, neat, and colorful casual clothes and had the latest in athletic footwear. When he got the idea that he wanted a cowboy hat and boots, someone went right out and bought them for him. He really looked handsome tooling down the corridors in his western attire.

It took me quite a while to get the hang of dressing Jim. His body was inert and his limbs offered no resistance. I had to find ways to dress those limbs quickly and efficiently. I had dressed babies and dolls but they didn't have arms and legs that flopped. The nurses knew all the tricks, but most of them did not talk to me or help. We worked it out and got the hang *of it though, and soon it was Jim who was first down to physical therapy in the morning.*

Physical therapy was so very important because it was there that Jim would work to get back as much movement as he could get.

From physical therapy he would go to lunch. There he was taught to eat by himself. That was very hard for all paralyzed persons. I wasn't supposed to help him and some days I wondered if he would ever get enough to eat. He would get discouraged after a few bites and want to quit. Actually, I think he just wanted me to help him. How hard it was to refuse to help! One of the hardest things of my entire life was refusing to help Jim when I knew he could learn to do it himself. So many tears were shed by both of us when he would ask for help and I had to refuse. Was Jesus crying too?

After lunch, Jim went to occupational therapy. It was there he learned to use prosthetic devices for eating, turning pages in a book, playing games, and even to do a little artwork. I have a little lion pin that he made for me with his mouth stick. It is one of my most precious pieces of jewelry.

Joni Erickson Tada won't find any competition here!

*Evenings were spent in recreation. There were many groups
who came to help the men pass the evenings. We seemed to
have our own groups though. Christ was so faithful through
His Body. We always seemed to have people around to cheer
and to comfort us.*

One day during some free time, I was going down the
hall in my wheelchair past the nurses' lounge. I lost my bal-
ance and slumped over sideways in my chair. I couldn't get
back up by myself and so I looked around for some help.
All I needed was for someone to push me back up straight
in my chair. I could see that there was a nurse sitting in the
lounge on her break having a cup of coffee. She saw me and
knew that I needed help. When she didn't volunteer, I po-
litely asked her if she could push me back up in my chair.

She said briskly, "Not now! I'm on my break. I'll get to you when I'm done." Needless to say, I was shocked and hurt by her response. I felt as though I must have been a tremendous burden not only to her, but also to my mother and everyone else in the world. Eventually, someone did come along and help me. But I was already devastated. I went to the recreational room where I could be by myself. There I was, starring blankly out the window at the freeway below, wondering why this had happen to me. I was angry and depressed, and my faith was being tried severely. It seemed like the enemy was attacking me in every conceivable way. I didn't think that it could get any worse, but it did.

Very early the next morning, my faith was challenged to its very core. One of the things that my mother tried to do while I was in the hospital was encourage me with Scripture verses. She challenged me to memorize them and even wrote some out and plastered them on the wall by my bed, including Isaiah 40:31. "But they that wait upon the Lord shall renew their strength. They shall mount up with wings as eagles. They shall run and not be weary, and they shall walk and not faint." Now, having Scripture verses plastered on the wall was not a very common sight in the VA. More often you would find things that revolved around immorality and licentiousness, such as girly pictures. It was obviously that I was a Christian. In fact, the other guys in the ward called me "the Reverend."

Well, early that morning before I was even awake, the ward psychiatrist visited me. He was concerned that I wasn't dealing well with the reality of my circumstances. He thought my Christianity was just a crutch and that I needed to get rid of it and act like the rest of the guys on the ward.

God would never help me if I didn't help myself first. I would never adjust properly to life in a wheelchair if I continued living in this fantasy world of faith in God. How could the Lord help me anyway? Get Real! Face facts!

What a joke! The other guys on the ward were boozers who went to Go-Go Bars till all hours of the night, smoked their brains out, cussed at the nurses, skipped therapy sessions, and were just plain disorderly. And that's what the doctor wanted me to be like? I guess he thought that they were really dealing with their disabilities in an appropriate way. But not me! I went to Bible studies, memorized verses, tried to be kind to the nurses, and went to all of my therapy sessions on time. I guess he thought that this was bad!

Nevertheless, he was very assertive and forceful, and our conversation really shook me up. Later that morning, when my mom and dad came in, they found me crying and I told them what happened. I thought I must have done something wrong. My dad went to talk to the ward psychiatrist immediately. I'm not sure what Dad said to him, but the shrink never talked to me again. I have often wondered about that man, so steeped in his humanism that he would openly call good evil and evil good. I feel sorry for him and I have often prayed that the truth of the gospel would touch his heart.

I know what Doug said to him because I was there. In spite of his infirmity, he gained a strength from the Holy Spirit that was incredible. His righteous anger just blazed from his whole body. He told that man a lot of things about our faith in Christ. And most of all, he told him to stay away from his son forever! Strangely enough, although his job required him to

council all the men, he never came back to Jim's little corner of
the ward.

The time at the VA was filled with long, dark days. I was
introduced to wheelchairs, prosthetic devices, physical
therapy, occupational therapy, and all kinds of other things
that just reminded me of my handicap and helplessness.
Though my mom and dad and friends continually tried to
encourage me in the Lord, I sank further and further into
depression, and I started running from the Lord as fast and
as far as I could. Yet, as I look back, I can see that God was
providing for my family and me in very real and significant
ways. He provided a house for my family to rent that was
easily made accessible for me. That made it possible for us
to spend Christmas of 1980 together in a real home. He
provided many caring people from the local churches to
support us spiritually and emotionally. There were men like
Gus who brought me gentle, spiritual encouragement and
a chocolate milkshake every day to help beef me up a little.
A young man named Scott came to the hospital just to spend
time with me. We played games and he challenged me with
my German skills. God provided a youth group that temporarily moved their Wednesday night Bible study to the
hospital so that I could attend. God provided Ginnie and
Carl and Jeanne for my mom during those long, lonely nights
in a strange house when my dad was back in Medina, Ohio
getting chemotherapy for the cancer that had returned with
a vengeance. The list could go on and on. God's family was
a very important part of our lives in those trying days. Yet,
in spite of all that, I was still angry and unwilling to submit
myself to God's plan for my life.

One night, the youth group decided to take me to a Christian film entitled, *Joni,* about a girl who, like me, was in a wheelchair. She had been in a diving accident and had broken her neck in much the same way I had. Joni was living her life for the Lord in her wheelchair. I'm sure that they thought I would be encouraged by this film. But I wasn't! I hated it! I thought she had given up. I was determined that I would walk again, and I knew that God could heal me if He wanted to. I wasn't going to give up so easily. So I continued to hold out on God and demand that He heal me before I would surrender my life to Him. (Little did I know what a significant role this film would play in my life in the future.)

While I was at the VA in Wisconsin, my dad's health began to deteriorate again. The cancer was back with a vengeance, this time in his bones and his lungs. I'm sure that the stress of having a son go through such difficult and overwhelming trials was a contributing factor to the reoccurrence of his cancer. The burden and demand that this put on my mother was almost unbearable. While she was caring for her son in Wisconsin, her husband was undergoing chemotherapy in Cleveland, Ohio. Dad would come back and forth as often as he could, but he was steadily getting weaker. He stayed by my side though, often sitting in a straight chair by my bed holding my hand or just touching my foot, praying that the feeling would come back. He was in great pain, but no amount of pleading from my mom or anyone else could persuade him to leave. Something had to be done. Mom couldn't take care of both of us. She had to be at the hospital by 7 a.m. or I would be in bed until she came. She had to be with my dad, too, who now needed hospitalization. It was a big problem.

The biggest problem here was financial. There were many wonderful facilities for rehabilitation in Ohio. However, they are all very expensive and usually are paid for by insurance. Jim's primary medical insurance, because he was in the military, was a military VA hospital. To pay for rehab privately was not within our capabilities. The military was in sympathy with our situation though, and were willing to work with us. There was attached to our own auto insurance, a medical payment that we hadn't used because the physical therapy of the VA in Wisconsin was provided.

Now we were in need of a private facility so we decided to use that policy. A facility at the Ohio State University in Columbus was considered very good. Columbus was only 90 miles from Medina. That was close enough that Jim could get home every weekend. It was decided that he would be airlifted there. This time I did not fly with him. I took my dear husband home. I knew in my heart that he was going home to die. I had to be there for him. This time I had to trust in the Lord to take care of my son. It tore me apart to leave him to the care of strangers. I had seen what the care of the nurses in Wisconsin was like. Would he be neglected in the new facility? At least now he was able to breathe on his own and could get around somewhat in a wheelchair. He was beginning to get stronger and to be able to fend for himself a bit.

Eventually it was determined that I would be moved to the spinal cord rehabilitation center at the Ohio State University in Columbus, Ohio. There were a number of advantages to this move. First, it was much closer to home, so mom could travel back and forth more easily, and I could go home for the first time since my accident. Second, there were patients my age there. Third, I had friends attending the Ohio State University who could come and visit me. And fourth, I would be able to continue my own schooling as part of my rehab. All of these factors made the choice easy, and in March of 1981, five months after my accident, I was moved into a semi-private room alongside another young man by the name of Steve. He was a year younger than I was, and he was a Christian. What a refreshing change!

This was such a change. As I said before, every patient was up and attending breakfast in a communal dining room. Even if the patient was in a prone position, he had to attend every meal. At the new rehab center they did not tell us that there was no hope. They told us that they saw miracles every day. The patients were focusing on getting to do more and more things, not concentrating on getting adjusted to what they couldn't do. This positive attitude made all the difference in the world to me and to everyone else concerned. What a change! In addition, the new rehab facility was a smoke free facility. Best of all, Jim was put in a room with another young Christian with whom he could share and do things.

Do things they did, too. He and Steve were always getting into trouble. They took off in their wheelchairs and found their way into the tunnels that connected every building on the Ohio State Campus. They wheeled around into every forbidden area they could find just to be mischievous. One day when I came to get Jim for the weekend, I found both of them wheeling around the halls, each with a girl in his lap!

At the Ohio State rehabilitation center I was able to see that life could go on. I got my own wheelchair. Boy, was that ever a contraption. It had an automatic, flip-up head-rest that made the chair look humongous. It was too wide for me, and didn't look good. I felt like calling it "Jim's Jalopy." But there was nothing I could do about it because it was new and custom-made. I was jealous though. Steve had a sleek-looking, nice, narrow chair, nothing like the contraption I had. I also got a van that had ramps so that I could get in and out. Putting the ramps on and off was a pain, but it was better than nothing. I had friends from high school who were now attending OSU and would come and visit me and take me out. I also started to develop some good relationships with the staff. They were very kind and helpful. One of the things that I enjoyed most was getting to know the student interns. I was a guinea pig for student nurses, student occupational therapists, and student physical therapists. I would often pretend they were hurting me just to give them a hard time. But the thing I enjoyed most was going home.

Getting Jim the 90 miles home every weekend and back again on Sunday could have been a real trial, but there were so many people who offered to make the drive for us. I will always be grateful for them. To accommodate the wheelchair, we bought a used van that we had converted to handicap use by simply getting two heavy boards to prop up on the doorframe. Jim teetered up those boards while one of us stood on the end and prayed nothing would slip. Most of the time we had help with the drive, but JD, Jackie, or I had to make the trip sometimes. The first time I had to do it myself was really scary. The van had no safety features or tie downs for Jim in his chair. Also, I was very new at driving a big vehicle like a van. On the way home I put on the brakes too hard and over Jim went. I was frightened out of my mind. Fortunately, we were near a rest stop and I could get off the interstate to right him again. What a sight we often were. Usually I would be crying and Jim would be patiently trying to calm me down as I struggled to cope with the heavy wheelchair or the big van ramps or some other catastrophe.

Those first few trips home were quite adventurous. We had no idea what to expect, so of course, we tried to prepare for everything. Even though I would only leave for the weekend, we packed so much stuff that the van resembled an ambulance filled with all kinds of medical supplies. I could hardly get in. Learning the best way to ride was also a challenge. A number of times I flipped over backwards in my chair. We learned very quickly that stabilizing my chair was a good idea. When I got home, there were more obstacles to face. We lived in a split-level house with lots of stairs. It was a good thing that my younger brother was big and strong because he had to do a lot of lifting. I even got rug burns answering the phone once. For some reason (I can't remember why) I was laying on the floor when the phone rang. It was for me, but I had no way to get to the receiver. Those were the days before portable phones. Just then, an ingenious idea popped into my head. I instructed mom to just grab me by the ankles and drag me to the phone. It was working great until I started to feel a burning sensation on my shoulder blades. But, in spite of all the difficulties and complications, it was good to be home. I was able to

see my friends, go to church, and most of all, spend time
with my dad.

*It was wonderful to be home again and to have my family
together again. All my children were home at least on weekends except for John. He was still in the Air Force but he snagged
a military ride to Cleveland whenever he could. It was also
very hard to have both Jim and Doug in wheelchairs.*

*Doug, by this time, could hardly get around. He had lost
so much weight and was so frail. I used to think of a mighty
tree when I would hug my husband. He always seemed to be
so strong and sturdy, a bulwark against any insecurity or problems that would come our way. He was our protection against
the world, but now all that had changed. I had to help him in
every way. I had to take care of him. I had to be the protector
and provider for this family. I found the weight of the responsibility very heavy.*

*Jackie and JD were my salvation in those days. They helped
in so many ways. They both helped physically with Jim and
with Doug. Jackie stayed home most of the days while I went
back to work. Then she went off to Akron University in the
afternoons and evenings after I got home. She had given up
being a lady geologist and was now studying to be a teacher
like her mom and grandmother. She was an excellent nurse
for her dad even though caring for him was really difficult
now, she was patient and kind, rubbing his back and reading
to him when he could listen. Her compassion for her father
was so loving. I was and am so grateful for my beautiful daughter.*

*JD was finishing his 11th grade work; but he took over all of
Doug's jobs around the house, willingly and with capability*

too. I have so often felt sorry about JD's last high school years. He had to grow up to be a man; and he had to do it without his mother or father's help. No one was home to watch his football games or to watch him as he played on the tennis team. No one was there to go to his choir activities as they were for his brothers and sister. He had to go through that alone, plus see to his father's duties, which were many. Jackie's car was always breaking down and he would have to rescue her from Akron U. Doug's old car seemed to be pretty faithful, but it required maintenance, too. In addition, several years earlier we had purchased two houses in Akron that we fixed up and rented out. JD had to deal with all the troubles of being a landlord and keep those up too. For a seventeen-year old, that is a tall order, but he did it without complaint and did it well.

As I said before, John was in the military and had a family of his own to care for in California. He felt helpless and alienated from us and from all the troubles we were enduring. He was going through some real troubles of his own, but kept them to himself because he didn't want to add to my burdens. I am so sorry he had to go through pain without the loving support of his mother. I know he wished he could help more. I knew his heart, though, and his love for us.

The Lord blessed me with wonderful children and I praise the Lord everyday of my life for giving them to me.

The first weekend that both Jim and Doug were home was Easter. We had lots of visitors from the church and we were kept busy, but it still was a very hard time. Both Jim and Doug were in wheelchairs and our house was impossible for handicapped people. It was built on four levels plus a finished basement. We could only get the wheelchairs into the family room via the garage. To get to the living room and kitchen with a wheelchair, they had to go around the house to the back door. To get to the bedroom level JD had to carry them. The basement and the top floor den were not considered accessible at all.

The solution was to convert the family room into a bedroom for Jim. There was a half bath there; so when a hospital bed was installed, he could be quite comfortable. A hospital bed was also put into the master bedroom for Doug so he could be comfortable too.

Having my lovely home turned into a hospital facility was bad, but seeing my two beloved men both sitting in wheelchairs, nearly broke my heart once again.

Getting used to Jim's cares was tedious and often mortifying for both Jim and I. I would not get the leg bag on quite right and Jim would look down to see one very wet shoe. If the shoe was all that was wet, he was lucky. Sitting in church while a puddle grows on the floor is terribly humiliating. Actually, sitting anywhere and hearing a hissing sound while a puddle forms under your chair is beyond agony and sometimes becomes extremely funny. Jim has often been forced to laugh because the only alternative is crying. Besides the leg bag accidents, I have dropped him on the floor more than once and had to go for help. I could go on and on about the humiliation Jim has suffered at my hands while I was learning to care for him.

Depression, my dad's suffering, my relationship with my girlfriend Kim, and my relationship with God were the primary areas of struggle during these days. I saved some notes that I had written during my time at the Ohio State rehab center as a part of my occupational therapy sessions. I share these notes with you only because they reflect how I felt and what God was doing in my life. They are transparent and even somewhat embarrassing, but still they are a reminder to me of God's grace in the midst of very difficult circumstances. (By the way, I wrote these using a manual typewriter and a mouth stick, which was a 1 foot long piece of doweling rod with a rubber cap on one end and a mouthpiece on the other. I would put the stick in my mouth and poke at the keys on the typewriter. I looked like a chicken pecking the ground as I hunted for each key one at a time.) The first entry is dated May 18, 1981.

"This is the first time I've written anything since my accident on October 29, 1980. There has been a drastic change in my life, especially concerning the people I'm close to. There are three things that really have plagued me lately. One, I'm paralyzed from the shoulders down, with no sign of return. But, I hold onto the fact that God can heal me anytime.

Two, my dad is practically on his deathbed. He has cancer, and I claim the promise of God for him too, and know that if he does die he'll go to heaven because he's a born-again Christian. I feel so mad sometimes because he suffers so much. He's on morphine, which makes him incoherent. I would be crushed if he died, yet almost relieved that he wouldn't suffer any more and be in heaven.

Three, I just got dumped by my girlfriend this weekend, and that was a killer. I hurt so much inside. I know it's all because of my accident. She says it isn't. I'm crushed that she doesn't want me any more.

God, I pray every day for healing because I feel like I would be able to get her back and I could help with my dad. Now, I just feel like a burden. God, why does this have to happen to me? I'm not happy like this and I don't like myself. You've got to do something soon. My life is falling apart. I'm so bummed out. Please heal me God, I know you can. There's got to be something better for me than this. I hate it."

How it hurt to see Jim suffer so! I felt such resentment against Kim. I'm really sorry for that now. Had I trusted the Lord more, I would have known that He always works things out for the best for those who love Him. However, I couldn't help my feelings. I was hurt and Jim was devastated. I just couldn't understand how God could keep allowing so many things to hurt him. God had His plan and now I can look back and see that His way is so much better than any plan I had. Then, however, it just hurt almost more than I could bear.

May 19, 1981

"I made a new commitment to God. I am going to share Christ with more people. Evangelizing. I've already hit three people in two days."

May 20, 1981

"So far since yesterday not much has happened. I got to share with one of my roommates last night, who is an atheist. He received it all pretty well. He said he would ask me if he had any questions.

I talked to Mom last night and told her about Kim. It helped to talk to her. She told me my dad was back in the hospital getting a blood transfusion. It hurts so much to hear about those things. He's a good upstanding Christian."

May 21, 1981.

"I've really felt convicted lately about my need to share Christ with other people. I talked to a guy named Murray last night and he's the third person that suggested I go to a healing service. I'm still praying about it because I'm still not convinced, but I think the Lord is starting to answer my prayer. I know you can heal me, God. Please do it soon so I can help out at home. Dad's probably home from the hospital now with some new blood. God, please help me. I don't like myself and I don't like what's going on. I'm not happy and I need help. You are the only One that's always with me, and the only One I can always trust. Praise God."

May 22, 1981

"Last night I went all over campus with Sandy (she was a good friend that I graduated from high school with) and met all kinds of neat people. I think I'm going to like it here because there are no norms or standards. You can be anyone you want, and you're accepted that way.

Today is a beautiful day. I feel good about my relationship with Christ. I'm counting my many blessings and not looking at what I don't have."

June 1, 1981

"I'll be going home in a little under two weeks. Dad's still in the hospital. I don't think it will be long before he goes home. He'll love it up in heaven.

Things are shaping themselves so that I can concentrate on getting better. I still haven't found peace about

myself. But, sharing so much has really made me feel better."

June 11, 1981 (The day my dad died)
"I haven't written for awhile because I was in the main
hospital. They thought I had thrombophlebitis. I was over
there for three days. I'm on tobramycin for a urinary tract
infection. One good thing though, a lot of people came to
see me, including Bobby and Marti. I feel like they are getting to be good friends.

Dad is the same. God is letting him feel comfortable.
Thank you God!

Things are going okay between God and me, but I have
fallen away a little. Every time I try to make a big commitment, I fall farther away. I think I try too hard to do things
my way. It doesn't work.

I'm going home for the summer June 16."

That's the last thing I wrote. It was my mom's birthday,
and I had been trying to call home all day to wish her Happy
Birthday! I couldn't get through. That night as I was lying
in bed (it was about 11:00), J.D. and Kim walked into the
room. At first, I thought they were there to surprise me for
mom's birthday. But as I saw the expression on J.D.'s face, I
knew exactly why they were there. Dad had died. I was
numb at first. The only thing I could think of was that his
suffering was over, but why did it have to happen on my
mom's birthday? The next morning, they took me home for
the funeral. I can remember the viewing, all the friends who
came to wish us well, and the funeral service. It was a bittersweet time. Dad was gone, but he was no longer suffering

and he was with the Lord Jesus Christ. I didn't even cry until a few days after the funeral. That's when it all came to a climax. My tragic accident, the heart-wrenching breakup with my girlfriend, and now my dad's death on my mom's birthday, all within eight months, was more than I could bear. I felt like Job. I wondered if there was anything else that God could take from me besides my life. I was confused, hurt, scared, and mad at God. He could have prevented it all! But He didn't! And if God was going to be so cruel, I wasn't going to serve Him. So I quit trying, and for the next two years I lived life for me.

While Jim was trying to work things out in Columbus, we were trying to cope with things at home. Satan threw another dagger at me. The IRS called and said that they were to audit our last returns. They informed me that I would have to come to Akron with papers and returns from the last several years. The income tax was one area that was Doug's alone. I knew nothing about it nor did I want to know. In fact, in trying to shelter me from the difficulties of finances, Doug had left me ignorant of all our affairs. When the IRS demanded that I come with information I didn't have and did not know how to get; I rebelled! I just said, "I'm not coming." I knew that Uncle Sam did not react kindly to people who resisted their audits, but this was just too much! The woman reiterated her statement that I would <u>*have*</u> *to come. I burst into tears and cried again, "I'm just not coming! I don't care if you come to put me in jail. I'm not coming!" The poor lady continued her demand that I would have to come and I continued to refuse and finally hung up. God came to my rescue in the form of one of His servants though. He sent Jerry Gould, a CPA from our church to help. Jerry calmly called and got an extension for me and continued* to get extensions until he could work with me in getting the necessary papers. He held the IRS at bay for several months and then stayed by my side until the audit was over.

Doug, by this time, needed constant nursing at home. Since I had gone back to my job teaching at the high school, Jackie stayed with him during the day as a loyal nurse. He was heavily medicated for pain and he wasn't always coherent anymore. He would tell Jackie that there were people in his orange juice and become very agitated. She patiently calmed him and somehow kept him that way until I would get home from teaching. She had a lot of support from the many friends from the church. Pastor Wolfe was so faithful to call every day. Many of Doug's brothers in Christ would come to pray with him or to read the Scripture. That seemed to be very soothing to him. One thing that amazed Jackie was the prayer time. Doug would seem so out of it, but when he would pray with the men from the church, his incoherence would disappear and his prayer would come from his mouth both steady and wise. The Holy Spirit was truly and obviously at work in him. Finally, he had to be hospitalized again. The hospital was not a good solution. He just wanted to be home. Whenever he was clear in his mind I wanted to be with him. He called one night at 4 a.m. and asked me over the phone if he was going to die. I just told him, "I will be right there." The hospital was only two blocks away and I was there within ten minutes; but in that time the clear headedness was gone. I had lost him to the medication. Therefore, when day school was out and my work year was over, I made arrangements for him to come home.

He came home on my birthday, June 11, 1981. The ambulance brought him home and the attendants kindly got him settled in the hospital bed. They hooked him up to a machine to deliver oxygen, instructed me on its delivery and his other medications and after making him comfortable, they left. I stayed by Doug's side, but he didn't wake up at all. I walked over to check the oxygen and then back to the bed. Doug barely raised his hand and I took it in mine. Then he got an expression on his face that I will never forget. He had this extraordinary look of wonder on his face. It was a look of such surprise, but not one of fear—just wonder. At that moment he left me and I know he went to be with the Lord. I was truly alone. My husband of thirty-one years was gone. I was left alone with all these troubles and my lifetime helpmate had deserted me. I can hardly believe my feelings at that time. I was angry with him for dying!

Jackie and I sat on the stairway crying as the ambulance which so recently had left, made the trip back. They asked if we wanted them to try to resuscitate; but we declined. Doug was now with his Lord and out of his pain. We just had to trust that the Lord would see us through the rest alone. JD went down to Columbus to bring Jim home and the extended family and all our friends began to gather.

God was faithful. He always is. Pastor Wolfe helped us through a beautiful funeral ceremony. He helped us all see that death for those in the Lord is a graduation celebration and that we could be happy our dad was no longer suffering. It was encouraging, but so hard too. As my sons and Doug's brothers carried my dear husband's coffin to the gravesite, they all walked so straight and tall; while Jim, in his wheelchair, tried to keep his hand on one corner of the coffin and do his part to carry his dad to his last resting place. I thought my heart would break and never mend again.

The next few weeks were very hard; but God, in His goodness, kept His people there. My brother came to stay for six weeks. He enlarged the door so Jim could get in the house easier and made several other modifications for our convenience. It was so good just to have him there with me.

Doug 's friends from the church rallied around also. One of them helped me with the insurance. I had been making payments on the house, a boat loan, and a car loan. He looked over our insurance and found that all those payments were not necessary now. He got the overpayments back for me.

One of John's friends came to stay for a couple of weeks. That man never stopped. He fixed everything around the house that had needed fixing since time began. I think he had his eye on Jackie but he certainly was a help to me.

The father and brother of Jackie's best friend got a crew together and poured a sidewalk from the garage to the back door so Jim wouldn't have to bump his way around on the wet, muddy grass. One volunteer in that sidewalk crew was to fall in love with my daughter and become my son-in-law.

For weeks the church ladies brought in meals. I think perhaps that that is why my brother stayed so long. He loved all those excellent meals.

Running from God

As you can see, I was a mess! I was desperately looking for ways to relieve the pain of living life in a wheelchair. Yet, at the same time I was turning away from the only One who could really help me. I am ashamed of many of the things that I did during this time of my life. I turned from God to the world and to many of the things that the world says will ease your pain. But none of it worked. It only covered the pain temporarily, then made it grow worse.

Satan never gives up. He flew another arrow right at us right after the loss of our dad. We received a letter from the Air Force that frightened us down to the depths of our beings. The letter stated that since Jim had received extensive medical care from them, they should be entitled to any insurance monies that had come to us as a result of the accident.

We hadn't received much from insurance. Colorado had a 'no-fault' insurance law that did not place fault on the woman who had run the red light. Even if that law had not been in place, she was not insured and she had no money. Therefore, there was no insurance compensation except through our own family car insurance.

One of Doug's "friends," a lawyer, told me he would take care of everything. I trusted him to do so. When I finally got to see him and talk to him, he said that there was no way we could collect anything for Jim, who had been so gravely injured. There was a small $50,000 claim we could make and he had done that for us. Then he gave us the bill for his services and that was $35,000. That was quite a big percentage of a very little compensation for Jim's total handicap. The Air Force letter said they were entitled to the medical compensation we had discussed earlier plus anything we had previously received including what the lawyer had taken. All of it had been used to pay for Dodd Hall rehab services. I was devastated and didn't know what to do. I had no money to give them and no place to get any.

I decided to write to my congressman and tell him the whole story. I certainly did not want to involve the lawyer again. If he did get the Air Force to forget the money, he would take most of it for his trouble. I told the whole story as well as I could in my letter and sent it off. Within two days I had a call from a General. This had to be top priority! He assured me that the Air Force had no intention to cause one of their service-connected men any distress. He apologized profusely and asked that I tell Jim how sorry they were to give him grief. He said a check would be in the mail that day for our relief. Within two days I had received the check to take care of hospital payments. I did not tell the lawyer about it either.

God was so good to us financially. He took care of us seemingly on the very day that we needed help. The Bible tells us that He never gives us more than we can bear. I think financial worries might have been a burden we couldn't handle over and above everything else. We never had to worry financially about anything for very long. I can't imagine the stress financial worries would be; if added to the pressure we were already under.

I praise our government, too, for doing some things right. They really do take good care of the men injured while in service. In spite of our bad experience with the nurses in Wisconsin, we have found that most of the VA hospitals are run with efficiency and compassion. The VA has been very good to provide Jim with any equipment he asks for and they have compensated him fairly for his daily living requirements too. Praise the Lord for our country. Our government has its faults, but it is still the best one there is.

That summer, after Dad died, I came home to try out all of the things that I had learned in rehabilitation. My folks had a summer home in Canada on an island where we had practically grown-up. We spent every summer up there from

85

the time I was four years old. It was definitely a haven of familiarity and security in my fragile world. It was a natural place to go for some therapeutic rest and relaxation. So, we packed up our stuff and headed off to Canada. We didn't even know how we would get me in my wheelchair across the river to the island (no cars are allowed on the island and the only way over is by boat), or how we would get into the cottage (it had a few steps which we hoped to remedy with a temporary ramp). But we went anyhow. I'll never forget the surprise we received when we got there. As the cottage came into sight, we saw the entire population of the island, longtime friends, waiting for us to arrive on the ferryboat. They were all standing around the front of the cottage hiding from us what they had done. They had cut a hole into the side of our cottage, installed a new door, and built a ramped deck for me to use. They had it decorated with a ribbon and a "Welcome Home" sign. When we arrived, there were a lot of tears, hugs, and condolences. It saved us all; me, my mom, and all my siblings, from the agony of meeting these people one-by-one and going through the sympathy and tears over and over again. We got it all out at once with everyone. For me, in the wheelchair, there was not the embarrassment that overcomes some people when they meet someone who no longer is able to shake hands, hug, or walk. Then they had a big party for us just to welcome us home. They'll never know what an encouragement that was to us.

Our happiest memories were of being on the island; so, in spite of the overwhelming difficulties and sadness, we determined to go there. By we, I mean Jackie, Jim, JD and myself, because John was still in California with his family.

We had no idea how we would get Jim into the cottage or even over to the island in a boat. He was in a heavy motorized wheel-

chair, not one you could lift or wheelie onto a ferry or up the steps to our front door.

Nevertheless, we resolved to go. We had advised my brother-in-law, Bill, who had a cottage there also, of our arrival so we would have some help getting Jim across the water.

In a way, I dreaded going back. The endless repetition of the amenities, the embarrassment and discomfort for Jim, the obvious pain of our dear friends and neighbors, was a difficult process to go through. I expected to go over the same phrases again and again and knew I would cry with each repetition to the folks on the island. Sometime we had to face it, though.

Above all, there was the problem of getting Jim in and out of the cottage. The wheelchair is big and heavy to manage manually, but we figured we could improvise and rig up some kind of ramp to get it in and out. It wouldn't be easy for Jim, but we'd cross that bridge when we got to it.

Bill, my brother-in-law, met us with the ferry with several men to help get Jim on. When we arrived at our dock we had the most touching greeting I could ever describe. There in our front yard were ALL our friends and neighbors from up and down the island. Behind them was a new deck, a ramp, and a new door sized to accommodate Jim's chair. My beautiful neighbors had cut a hole in the side of my cottage and made accommodations for my son. They engineered the building of the ramp and probably questioned the wisdom of cutting a hole in someone else's cottage without permission. I want all involved to know that they could have cut a hole in the roof to lower Jim in, and I wouldn't have cared. Their thoughtfulness and love were all I cared about. I have a picture of all the men working together in the hot sun, trying to get this thing done before our return.

The love extended that day was mixed with sorrow and tears. Everyone wept together and hugged and offered their heartfelt regards plus their happiness at seeing us all again. No one was embarrassed or at a loss for something to say. Our mutual sorrow said it all. We simply loved one another.

My throat closes and my eyes fill with tears every time I think of that day. I just can't explain adequately my gratitude. It will remain in my heart forever as a tribute to God's grace when He blesses us with good friends.

That summer at the island was both a tremendous joy and a very difficult experience. I had grown to love that place very much. It was a kid's paradise. My memories were of playing in the water all day, swimming and skiing, and just goofing around on whatever we could find that floated.

Sometimes we played on things that didn't float so well, like patched up old boats that took on water faster than we could bail. We had so many tree-forts that no tree was safe from our exploits. At night, we played hide-n-seek, kick-the-can, or just hung out around a bonfire. We were always doing something. But now, that was all changed. I couldn't swim on my own. I couldn't ski anymore. I couldn't even ride in the boat. I couldn't climb a tree. I couldn't dress myself. I couldn't even eat, comb my hair, or brush my teeth without help. I was trapped in a body that couldn't do a thing.

One of the greatest difficulties for me that summer was watching my family go water skiing, a daily ritual for the Fritzes. One morning as I was on the dock watching J.D. ski, I was overwhelmed with sadness and anger. I wanted to ski so badly that I could feel it—the wind in my face, the coolness of the water spraying against my ankles as my ski glided over the surface, the exhilaration of rounding a buoy on a slalom course and cutting across the wake as hard as I could to catch the next one. I couldn't handle it. I turned around, bolted off the dock and down the tractor trail as fast as I could. I didn't even tell anyone that I was leaving. Of course, when they all got back they had no idea where I was. J.D. eventually came running down the tractor trail looking for me. When he found me I was crying and I told him that I just couldn't handle it anymore. I wanted to ski too. I was sick and tied of being so helpless and such a burden. He put his arms around me (got me all wet) and cried with me. He said, "Jim, we'll get through this together! Just don't give up." Again I have to say that I thank God for my family. Each and every one of them was a tremendous encouragement and support for me when I needed them.

Not everything at the cottage was so emotionally difficult. In fact, there were also some quite humorous things I got myself into. I love to go swimming. It feels so cool and refreshing. So it was important to find an easy way to get me in and out of the water. We had a hoist out on the dock for the boat. It seemed like there ought to be some way to hook me to the hoist so I could be lowered into the water and lifted back out again. One day, I was watching our neighbors sail their catamaran (a sailboat with two pontoons). One of the sailors had on a life vest that clipped to a cable that was attached to the top of the mast. This allowed him to stand on the side of the boat and lean out over the water as far as he could, putting his entire weight on that cable. The farther he leaned out, the harder the cable pulled the mast and the sail into the wind and, consequently, the faster they went. I thought to myself, "If that vest can bear that kind of stress, maybe I can use it to clip me to the hoist." We immediately set to work testing our theory. Mom helped me get strapped into the life vest, wheeled me out onto the dock, and clipped me to the hoist. We were immediately confronted with another problem. The hoist would not pivot from its position over the water to a position directly over me on the dock. Our only choice was to start cranking me up to see what happened. As soon as the cable was bearing enough of my weight to free me from the chair, I swung out over the water and immediately flipped upside-down. My arms and legs were flying all over the place as I swung back and forth. I looked like a spider hanging from a thread, an upside-down spider. I was too heavy to try to pull back in over the dock, so the only option was to start letting me down into the water. The only problem with that was that I was going headfirst. Now I can hold my breath pretty long, but not that long. It didn't take us long to realize that we needed some help. Mom ran to call in the cavalry while I hung upside-down turning redder and redder. When help finally came, all they could do was laugh. It took some doing, but eventually I was freed, both from the harness and my stupidity. I took the vest back to where it belonged and never considered using the hoist again.

In spite of the good times, the anger in my heart and the depression I was experiencing continued to grow worse and worse as I ran from God. I knew that He could change things for me and I was mad because He wasn't doing what I wanted. I resorted to some things that, now as I look back, I am not very proud of. One of them was drinking. Alcohol was one of those subtle devices that made it easy to temporarily escape from the pain of my circumstances. It was never a permanent solution though. The pain always returned. It didn't matter how I tried to escape, whether through alcohol, parties, or whatever, the pain always returned. There was never a permanent solution in what the world had to offer. In fact, the pain grew worse as I ran farther and farther from God.

I was well aware of the pain Jim felt and to some extent, so was the rest of the family. I, however, saw it the closest. At night, when I got Jim ready for bed, he would lie there with a completely withdrawn expression. It was clear that he was feeling emotion that he couldn't or wouldn't express. I always came back later to see if he had gone to sleep. He never had. He would lie in bed and shake and cry and ask me to lie down on top of him. He wanted to feel his body. He felt like he didn't have a body anymore and the pressure of my body on his gave him a sense of physical being. I wished I could just transfer my sense of being into him. I wanted to will my sense of movement into his body. All I could do was just hold him and love him with all of my being. All of this time my prayers were for healing, nothing else would be acceptable to me.

After the summer of 1981, I returned to Dodd Hall to evaluate how things had gone at home over the summer and to complete my rehabilitation. That fall I enrolled in classes at the Ohio State University. I decided to major in secondary education with an emphasis in physics and computer science. My mom, who was a high school teacher, worked with a guy who was in a wheelchair and who taught on the high school level too. He had written me a letter soon after my accident, which was inspirational to me. He was a good role model for me. I include the letter because his own words say it better than I ever could.

Dear Jim,

I've been going to write for a week now. But I've put it off and put it off—worried that I wouldn't say the right things. Tonight I decided I'd just have to have faith that the right words would come or that somewhere between the lines you would see the meaning of what is in my heart.

Your family means more to me than you probably know. If there are better folks than your parents, I just haven't met them. I've always felt the goodness in them was clearly present in their kids. I don't just like your family - I love them. And right now I feel about as close to you as is possible. Two thousand miles of distance seems nothing. I've felt your pain, be-

wilderment, and frustration. I've hurt more than I thought I could hurt inside. And you are in my prayers around the clock. I know that you have been battered, but have faith the Lord will hold you gently in His hands.

My favorite quote is from an anonymous prayer found on a battlefield after the Civil War:

I asked God for everything,
So that I might enjoy life.
Instead God gave me life,
So that I might enjoy everything.

God has given you life—a second time. You are surrounded by a family who loves you, and a whole town full of folks who are calling on God to take special care of Jim Fritz. I could fill this page with the names of teachers and students who care and pray for you.

I wish there were some magic words. We all do. Just hang tough my young friend. Your patience and faith will heal you as quickly as anything medicine has to offer. This much I can say, "Through all of the tough times yet to come there is much to learn if you are open. You will be stronger and more aware of life because of your pain and the pain you share with those who love you." And by the way, Jim—Let them share it—they need to and want to. And none of us can do it all alone. Take care.

God bless always,
Rich Clevidence

Rich had been through everything I had. He knew what it was like. He had become a successful teacher and coach.

I liked the idea of teaching. I liked physics and computer science, so at least I had a direction to go. Eventually, I finished my rehabilitation, got an apartment in Columbus, Ohio, and settled down to finish my schooling.

One of the biggest challenges for me to face had to do with learning to rely on others because I was so dependent. I couldn't live on my own, so I had to find people who could attend to my needs. God worked here also. My first attendant was Ron Booker, a young man who came from my home church in Medina, Ohio. Ron just wanted to be a blessing. He learned all the things necessary to be my attendant and came to Columbus to help me move on with my life. For the next 18 months, Ron helped me get up in the morning, go to school, eat my meals, do my schoolwork, go to bed, and do whatever else I needed. On the weekends, we would go back to Medina and Mom would take care of me while Ron had the weekends off. Now, that may not sound like much, but week after week, it gets to be a pretty demanding job (even though I don't think I'm a particularly demanding person, ha ha!).

School was also a daunting task. How was I ever going to be able to accomplish the work that needed to be done when I was so unable to do anything for myself? How would the other kids respond to me? How would I get to class? How would I take notes? How would I write papers? All of these concerns made going back to school seem an insurmountable impossibility. But I really wanted to go back to school and knew that I had to if I ever wanted to get on with my life. I got some great advice from my quadriplegic friend, Rich. He told me to do two things. One, take some carbon paper to class for someone to put under their notes so that I could have a copy. And two, sit next to the pretti-est girl in class with your carbon paper. I took his advice and off to school I went.

Most of the time the other students were very willing to help me out. Only once did a girl tell me that she didn't want to help. That hurt, but I got over it and went on to the next girl. (Let me add just one side note here. That advice served me very well in the years to come. It was by heeding that advice that I met my wife. I'll tell you more about that later.) So, with my carbon paper in hand and determina-tion in my heart, I began the educational process again—1 1/2 years at OSU, four years at Appalachian Bible College, five years in graduate school, and five more in post-gradu-ate school. That's a lot of school, and I may not have been able to go as fast as usual, but with determination and God's enablement, the task was accomplished.

During those days at OSU, I was still very sensitive to spiritual things. I knew I was running from God, but He was still very active in my life. I didn't like what He was doing and I didn't want to serve Him until He changed it, but I knew that He was the only One who could change it. On the weekends when I was at home, I would always go to church, the same little country church in which I was saved. I still hungered for God's Word, but I wasn't quite ready to submit to His will. I would witness to my unsaved friends, pray to God for healing, go to church, and then live like the world. I can't imagine that I was a very good testimony and I know that I was miserable inside, all because I was unwill-ing to submit myself to the Father's plan for my life.

I can remember praying every night along these lines. "God, I don't like my life the way it is. I don't like being in a wheelchair. I don't feel I can serve you like this, and frankly, I don't want to. But, I know that You can heal me. I know that You healed people in the Gospels and that the Apostles healed people in the Book of Acts, and I know that You are 'the same yesterday, today, and forever.' I know that You can heal me. And Lord, if You would heal me, I would serve You with the rest of my life. Just think of what a dynamic testimony my life would be if You would heal me! I would be able to tell everyone what a wonderful God You are. I would tell them that You healed me and that because of this I am Your servant forever. Please heal me God, and I will serve You with the rest of my life." That was pretty much the focus of my prayer life in those days. As you can see, it was quite selfish and theologically unsound. But God kept working in me and teaching me lessons that would soon alter the direction of my life forever.

After 1 ° years studying physics and computer science at OSU, I was lost. I had no idea what I wanted to do with the rest of my life. I couldn't see myself just plunking away at a computer, or even teaching on the high school level for the rest of my life. I only had one year to go in order to graduate, but I had no motivation whatsoever. It was now the Spring of 1983. I still didn't like my life, and I still didn't like what God was doing in it. The only answer was to quit. So, I quit. I discontinued the lease on my apartment, packed my things, and went home with no idea whatsoever what I would do.

While I was at home, a group of men from my church approached me with a proposition. They were making arrangements to have the film *Joni* shown in the Medina area. They wanted to promote it as much as possible, so they asked me if I would be willing to go to some of the local churches and local civic organizations to give a short promo concerning the film. Now, if you'll remember, I had seen the film before and absolutely hated it. They wanted me to promote the film about a girl who had come to grips with her handicap, while I was still struggling a great deal with mine. I had a second good reason to refuse: I didn't like to talk in front of people. But, they were my friends and it was hard for me to say no, so I consented. Little did I know that consenting to push this film would cause me to search myself to the depths of my soul.

After having given a short promo in a couple of civic organizations and churches, I was down to my last engagement. It was Saturday night and the next morning I was scheduled to speak in one of the local churches that I knew had unsaved people in it. As I was praying that night, I went through my routine requests for healing. I prayed that the Lord might heal me and make me a dynamic testimony for His Name. I said, "Lord, just think how tremendous my testimony would be if I could <u>stand</u> in front of my friends tomorrow morning. I would praise Your Name and testify to Your greatness. Please, heal me!" Then, I started to pray for those people to whom I would be speaking the next morning. I said, "Lord, I know that there are unsaved people in that church; people I know and love. Please make me the best testimony that I can be tomorrow!"

Those words struck me as they had never done before. My mind started to reel in a flurry of thoughts that I had never considered before. I started to ask questions. How would I be the best testimony in that church the next morning? (In my wheelchair.) Why did those men ask me to promote this film anyway? (Because I was in a wheelchair.) What was God trying to do in my life? (He wanted to use me in my wheelchair.) For the first time in almost three years, it dawned on me that God could use me, and wanted to use me, **IN MY WHEELCHAIR**. You can't imagine how significant that realization was. It meant that I wasn't useless. It meant that I wasn't without purpose. God had a wonderful plan for my life and He wanted to use me in a very special way. That night, I broke down and confessed my hard-heartedness and sin to God, and submitted myself and my life to Him, even if it meant spending the rest of it in a wheelchair. At that moment, God lifted the burden from my soul, and gave me that peace that passes all understanding (Philippians 4:7).

This was definitely a Romans 12:1–2 decision. Paul said, "I beseech you therefore, brethren, by the mercies of God, that you present your bodies a living sacrifice, holy, acceptable to God, *which is* your reasonable service. And do not be conformed to this world, but be transformed by the renewing of your mind, that you may prove what *is* that good and acceptable and perfect will of God" (NKJ). I was presenting my body to God for His work, which was my reasonable service.

My life changed dramatically. I no longer wanted to be conformed to the world. My language changed; my drinking habits ceased completely; my desires changed. They changed completely and radically. It was not a progressive thing, but a one-time decision to forsake those worldly things completely. My desire was to be transformed by the renewing of my mind and to be made conformed to the perfect will of God. I now wanted to live for Him regardless of the wheelchair. What a day that was! I can remember it as if it were yesterday. It had taken a long time, but I had finally come to grips with God's requirement that I submit to His will for my life. Now don't get me wrong. There are still times when I struggle with being in a wheelchair, but I have learned that God's grace is sufficient for those times (2 Corinthians 12:9–10).

In the summer of 1982, I decided to sell my house. With Jim's help, we would build a new house that would be fully accommodated to his handicap. Together we designed and built a lovely home. It was to be his house, but it had a part just for me, too. It was great therapy for both of us because it gave us a project to concentrate on and a sense of direction. A good family friend built the house and it was a labor of love for him. Because of this friend, we never once had to worry about whether it would be a quality house nor did we have the problems new house builders usually have. I loved the result of our efforts and so did Jim. Little did I know that he would never really live there.

A New Direction

What a wonderful change had taken place in me! Instead of running from God, I was now seeking His will. Unfortunately, I had no idea what His will for my life was. I dedicated the summer of 1983 to determining where to go next. With the council of my pastor, Rev. Harold Wolfe, I started looking into Bible colleges. Most of the schools that I had heard of were either inaccessible or unacceptable for other reasons. Only one option seemed to continually present itself—Appalachian Bible College. I had never heard of it before. I didn't know anyone who went there. The only contact I had with ABC was that Pastor Wolfe had heard the singing group from the College and was impressed with them. That's all I had to go on.

The fact that the school was in rural Southern West Virginia also bothered me. I wasn't sure I wanted to go to school that far from home. But, with no other options, I was finally persuaded to at least visit the college. I was reluctant for a number of reasons. First, who would take care of me? Second, what would I study there? Third, was it really accessible (a thing hard to imagine in the hills of West Virginia)? And fourth, what about all my friends and family back home, to whom I had become very attached? Despite my misgivings, a visit was scheduled two weeks before school started in August of 1983.

I'll never forget the total dismay I felt as we drove on campus the first time. You have to remember that my prior experiences with college were at the United States Air Force Academy and at the Ohio State University, two schools that were noted for their tremendous facilities. The first thing that I saw as I drove onto the campus at ABC was the "Upper Tin City," an affectionate name given to a small group of rusting trailers parked on the hillside for married students. Approximately 10 of them littered the hillside, all connected by a dusty dirt road weaving its way through the trailers. Next to the trailers stood two old Quonset huts that looked like they dated back to World War II. One served as the post office and the other as the maintenance garage, with the mandatory junk spread out around the building. Across the street from the post office was McCarrell Hall, the men's dormitory and the only building seen from the entrance that looked to be of recent vintage. As I came down the hill from the entrance, I saw Pipkin Hall, the main administration building, and Des Plaines Hall, the girl's dormitory. At this point, things started to look up just a little bit. Then, as I rounded Pipkin Hall, the rest of the campus came into view. It consisted of one building, Beukema Hall, which held classrooms. It was nice but seemed very lonely sitting all by itself on the hillside. I also could see a soccer field; below it was one large sinkhole filled with weeds, reeds, and smelly stagnant water; and the "Lower Tin City," another small group of trailers along a dirt road for married students. That was it. It was pretty dismal, and my first impression dictated the conclusion, "No Way!" I thought to myself, "You've got to be kidding!"

Then I met some of the people who made up Appalachian Bible College. They impressed me as kind, friendly, and interested in me as a person. They wanted to help me find God's will for my life, whether it meant attending ABC or not. When asked if they could accommodate me in a wheelchair and find someone to attend to my needs, Jeff Youell, the Admissions Director, answered, "**YES!** In letters 12 feet high." And yet, in spite of the difference that the people of ABC made, I still felt hesitant about the place. My strong dependence on my mom, my closeness to family, and the security I felt at home made thoughts of leaving incredibly frightening. How could I live dependent upon total strangers that far from home? I returned from that visit more confused than ever. Did God really want me to go to Bible college and, if so, what would I study? What would I do with the rest of my life?

I didn't have much time to make a decision if I was going to attend ABC that fall. I had no idea what to do so I called in the heavy artillery, my youth pastor. I can remember sitting with him literally all day long discussing the pros and cons of attending ABC. I knew that God was leading in that direction, but I wasn't sure if I was ready to step out on my own yet. The next Wednesday night, just three days prior to when the new freshman students reported to ABC, I remained undecided. I went to the Wednesday night prayer meeting with a great deal of turmoil in my heart. After an evening of intense struggle in prayer, I felt no closer to a decision than before. As I was leaving the church, Pastor Wolfe asked me if I had made a decision yet. I said, "No, I'm just not sure what to do!" I'll never forget his reaction. With a great deal of pointedness, which was totally unlike him, he sternly said, "Oh, why don't you just go?" I was totally taken back and surprised at his direct response. My first reaction was, "But, you just don't understand!" I went home angry and incensed at his lack of compassion and understanding. But, his directness was just what I needed. That night, God spoke to my heart and convinced me that I needed to go. The next day I called Pastor Wolfe and told him that I was packing my bags to go to Appalachian Bible College.

That next week was one of the most important of my life. The hurdles that my family and I had to overcome were incredible. It was a particularly hard week for my mother. We packed my van with everything we could think of that I would need: my clothes, my computer, my Bible, and all the myriad supplies a quad needs. We had no idea what to expect once we got there. The Director of Admissions had already made arrangements for one of the guys in the dorm to be trained to be my attendant. His name was Ken Davis. He already had a job at the mall that he needed in order to go to school. He would have to quit his job if he was going to work for me, but Mom couldn't guarantee him that I would stay long. After a night of prayer, Ken determined that he would take my offer, even if it was only temporary. He had no idea if he would be able to do the job or even like it, but he made the sacrifice just the same. Being so far from home, living in a dorm, having a new attendant who was a total stranger, being all by myself—everything seemed so new, so strange, and so scary! I felt so insecure that I wasn't sure I would be able to stay. After getting settled in and training Ken in everything that he needed to know to care for my needs, the time came for my mom to leave. Because I needed to keep my van to get around, the plan was for her to take a bus back to Medina, Ohio. I still wasn't convinced. I was scared, insecure, and emotionally stressed. Finally, my mom made a deal with me. I agreed to stay for four weeks and if I didn't like it after that, she would come and get me. She got on the bus and left. Little did I know that she cried the entire bus trip home, 7 hours straight. I didn't realize what a tremendously hard thing it was for her to leave me in the hands of total strangers. Yet, I praise God that He gave her the wisdom and strength to do so. If I was ever to have any measure of independence, it had to start then, or it would just have gotten harder and harder to make that separation.

Those four days that I spent at ABC getting Jim ready to stay there for a trial time, were four of the hardest days of my life. I'd rather go through birth pains 20 times in comparison to that separation. I realized that if Jim were to have independence and a modicum of normalcy in his life; it had to be on his own and not tied to his mother. However, that knowledge was in my head. He had been terribly hurt while off on his own. Could I chance letting that happen again? These people were all strangers and I would have to let go and rely on them. Jim would not be an hour away. He would be seven hours away! I couldn't get to him if he needed me. He couldn't even call me unless someone helped him.

Everyone at ABC was so kind, but it was the week before school was to start and there were no students on the campus, and most of the people were very busy hidden away in their offices getting their work done. We saw the staff at lunch only and that turned out to be a disaster the first day. Jim and I were going through the lunch line and it seemed like everyone was watching us. We were the oddity on campus—Jim in his chair and with his mother. We got the tray loaded for both of us and then I dropped the whole thing. Food and utensils flew everywhere. What an introduction to the whole faculty and staff of the school!

I was housed in the girls' dorm in a basement room that would not be used for students. The rest of the rooms had been prepared for the incoming students who had not yet arrived. I was the only person in the whole big building. It was very musty down there and lonesome and scary too. I opened the window for fresh air, but immediately had to close it again because something had fallen into the window well and died down there. I was the only inhabitant in that whole large dorm and down in the basement! This was not conducive to my peace of mind. It colored every aspect of my stay. I did not think I could ever leave Jim in this place.

Jim was put in the men's dorm with Ken Davis, who was to learn Jim's care and live with him in the dorm. They were the only residents there, too. I'm sure the big, vacant, quiet build-ing had an adverse affect on Jim, too.

The four days were intended as a training session for Ken, and also for Jim to ascertain if he could get around on the campus. I don't think I could have left Jim if it hadn't been for Ken's certainty that God really wanted him to do this for Jim. We felt strongly that we should not ask Ken to quit the secu-rity of his present job to take on the task of caring for Jim, because Jim was so uncertain about staying there for a whole semester (I was, too!). We expressed our concern to Ken and told him that quite likely Jim would stay two weeks, find it too difficult, and want to go home. Ken prayed about it that night and told us the next morning that he felt very strongly that the Lord wanted him to do this even if it was for only a few days. He just knew that he had to quit his job and try, because he felt called to do so. His confidence in the Lord's will was very encouraging to me. If he cared that much, I had to do my part and let him. I needed to do the Lord's will, too.

At the end of the four days, Ken proved to be very adept at Jim's care and they took me to the bus station in Jim's van. I boarded the bus for Akron and cried the entire seven-hour trip. I have no idea what all the other passengers thought. No one even asked, so I didn't have comfort there. Jim Imig picked me up at the bus station in Akron to bring me home to Medina and he had to look helplessly on while I cried all the way to Medina. I tried to have faith in what I knew to be the right thing. I just didn't have much faith right then.

I was certain that I would be going home in four weeks, a bad assumption as it turned out. I went through the next three weeks with the idea that it wasn't necessary for me to do any homework, study for any quizzes, or get involved much in any of the activities. But, God was still at work in my heart. After three weeks, I called my mom and told her that I still didn't like it and that I wanted her to come and get me the next week. I'm still not sure what happened to change my mind, but three days later I called Mom and said, "Okay, I'll stay for one semester, and that's it!" Obviously, I had a lot of catching up to do. By the end of the semester, though, I was hooked. I loved it at ABC. I loved the people, I loved the classes, I loved the friends I was making, and I loved the direction my life was taking. I told mom that I was staying for the entire four years to complete a degree.

Life Goes On

My four years at Appalachian Bible College were an incredible time of growth and spiritual enrichment. It was also a time that I had to make some major decisions in my life. It wasn't very far into my freshman year when the Lord confronted me with one of those decisions. In the winter of 1984, ABC had their annual missions conference. It was the first one that I had ever attended. One of the speakers was Mr. Norman Niemeyer, a veteran missionary from Trinidad/Tobago. He challenged us to be surrendered to the will of God with three key words: whatever, whenever, and wherever. Was I going to do whatever God wanted me to do? Would I be available whenever God wanted to use me? Would I go wherever He wanted me to go? The Holy Spirit was doing a mighty work in my heart during that conference. The night before the closing session, I spent an extended period of time in my room alone wrestling with God. When the closing invitation was given to those who wanted to commit themselves to full-time Christian service, I went boldly forward, knowing that the Lord was calling me to a lifetime of service.

It wasn't until my sophomore year that I would meet Kathy, my wife-to-be. Our first impressions of each other were less than flattering. She seemed so young to the mature 24-year-old that I was. I seemed arrogant and proud. We didn't really seem to have much in common, until we were both given the same Christian service assignment. We were to team-teach the Juniors at the local church that we attended. In order to get to know her better, I used the advice that was given to me way back when I first started OSU. I picked the prettiest girl (which she happened to be) in the lunch line and asked if she could help me with my tray. It didn't take long for me to realize that she was a very special girl, with many talents and a desire to serve the Lord. I can't praise the Lord enough for the wife that He has given me. She is the perfect helpmate; kind, compassionate, and fun to be with. We dated for the next three years and were married on June 13, 1987. I had just graduated from ABC and she had one more year to go, so we rented an apartment for one year so that she could finish. She went to school and I typed all of her papers, one key at a time!

I can't describe in any better way how the Lord can give a gift that is beyond your fondest dreams than to use my daughter-in-law, Kathy, as an example. Had I written out an order and

listed every requirement I hoped for, I wouldn't have come up with a wife for Jim that was as perfect as the one God gave me. She is a gift that becomes more precious with each passing year.

She has valiantly tried to fit into our adventurous family and has done many things she really would rather not do, just to

please us. She has shivered in fear, as we encouraged Jim to scuba dive. She's braved the deep in an inner tube, because we love to float down the river in the current at our summer home in Canada. She has taken to the air to travel commercially even though she is terrified of flying. She has been soft in answer, yet strong in conviction in all her dealings with the family. I hope she realizes how much I love her and appreciate God's giving her to me as a daughter-in-law.

When Jim went to meet her parents for the first time it was such a disaster. It is a wonder they ever saw one another again. Ron Eastwood, one of Jim's faithful friends, drove Jim to Pennsylvania to see Kathy and to meet her parents. They had a nice dinner and left to stay in a nearby motel because Kathy's house was inaccessible for Jim in his chair. Ron forgot to take out his contacts that night and the next morning, he could barely see. His eyes were swollen almost shut and very painful. He managed to get Jim dressed in . . . Jim, you should tell this story! It is funny and a really cute story but I can't tell it right!

It was a real mess, including me. You've heard of the blind leading the blind; well this was the quadriplegic leading the blind. When we woke up that morning, Ron's eyes hurt him so badly that he could barely open them. After trying in vain to soothe Ron's eyes enough to get them open, we decided that I would be his eyes and he would be my hands! Kind of like one of those symbiotic relationships; mutual dependence. We were supposed to be back over to Kathy's house around 10 am that morning, but I knew that we were going to be late. I called and told her that we'd probably need another hour. Boy, was that wishful thinking! I proceeded to talk Ron through everything that was necessary skipping as many of the none-essentials as we could. He kept his eyes closed, trying to save them for the 5-mile drive back to Kathy's house. 2 hours later I was up. I didn't look good, but I was up. I had on a T-shirt with a leather jacket over it because we couldn't handle a shirt. My hair wasn't combed. My face wasn't shaved. My teeth weren't brushed. Not exactly the best way to make a good impression on your girlfriend's parents. We checked out of the motel and loaded our stuff into the van, all the while I was Ron's eyes. By this time it was 1 p.m., but the worst is yet to come. We had hoped that by allowing Ron to keep his eyes closed all morning that he'd be able to negotiate the 5-mile drive ahead of us. I knew we were in trouble when the easiest way to the on ramp was down the left-hand berm of the road. We were traveling in the wrong direction. We made it to the on ramp. Ron was struggling tremendously to keep his eyes opened and focused on the road. I was trying to help by saying, "a little right, a little left," etc. We made it about 500 yards past the on ramp and could go no farther. I was barely able to talk him off the road and to a stop. There was no way we were going to make it all the way to Kathy's house like that. So there we were, a quad and a blind guy, stuck on the side of the road with no way to get help. We hadn't even been sitting there long enough to consider our options when a state trooper pulled up behind us to see what was wrong. I'm not sure what he thought of this pathetic twosome, but he took pity on us and said he'd drive us to our destination. In order to do that he had to call another trooper with a partner, so that he could drive the van and the other guy's partner could drive his cruiser. Before I knew it, three state cruisers were following us. Why the third one showed up, I'm not sure. Probably because he needed a good laugh. By this time it was 2 p.m. and Kathy and her family were starting to worry about us. It must have been quite a sight when we finally pulled up. A quad and a guy half blind in a van being driven by a state trooper followed by three other squad cars. It's a wonder her parents ever agreed to let me see her again.

Jim's marriage was a wonderful blessing for all of the family. We were so happy to see his happiness. We loved Kathy and all her family. I worried about their being able to cope with all of the problems attendant to paralysis. When Kathy's mother assured me that they felt the marriage was God's will, I felt better and decided I needed to take a lesson from her and lean more on the Lord. Kathy's parents are such godly people and such a testimony to the Lord's goodness. I praise God for them every day in my prayers.

Jim's graduation was another exciting milestone and a day for me to feel such pride in my son. How my heart thrilled as my beloved redhead wheeled down the aisle to get his diploma. It was even more gratifying to see Jim get the President's Award for "exemplary experience as a graduating senior." Pastor and Mrs. Wolfe brought me down for the graduation ceremony and I think Pastor took as much pride in the event as I did.

After Kathy graduated, we served as interns at Kathy's home Church in Salina, Pennsylvania. It was an invaluable time of exposure to the local church ministry. It was also fun to be so close to her family. I have been blessed with wonderful in-laws. During that time, it became evident to us that we were suited best for some kind of counseling-type ministry. It was the summer of 1989. We had just returned from a long trip to California for my brother's wedding. We were eagerly anticipating that the rest of the summer would be relatively uneventful and relaxing. One day, I received a telephone call from Dr. Daniel Anderson, the president of Appalachian Bible College. I had no idea what he wanted. After exchanging the usual pleasantries, he asked me a question that almost made me drop the phone. The Dean of Students was terminating his employment to go back into a local church ministry. Dr. Anderson wondered if I would be interested in temporarily helping to fill the gap. I had never considered working at ABC before. It was a place that I held in such high esteem that I never even thought it possible. When I hung up the phone and told Kathy, she could hardly believe it either. After much prayer, we determined that this was the Lord's will, and the arrangements for us to come to ABC for one year were made. My official title was "Acting Assistant to the Dean of Students." What a mouthful! It hardly fit on the doorplate. But what a privilege to serve at ABC, even if it was for only one year. After our first year was up, my position was made permanent and my title was changed to "Dean of Men" (much easier to fit on the doorplate). We have been here 12 years now. I am still the Dean of Men and Kathy serves as the Dean of Women. We love working with our students, seeking to help them grow in the grace and knowledge of our Lord Jesus Christ. I have been teaching a course on the Gospels and the Book of Acts for 11 years, and another course in Foundations of Marriage and the Family for 6 years. We praise God for allowing us to serve at such a special place; a place that we both love very dearly. So, a four-week promise has turned into over 16 years at Appalachian Bible College in one capacity or another. God is so good!

Let me just add a note of encouragement here for those of you who are trying to go through school with various kinds of disabilities. **DON'T GIVE UP!** I have earned a four-year Bachelor's Degree in Bible and Theology from Appalachian Bible College, a Master of Arts Degree in Religion from Liberty University School of Lifelong Learning, and a Doctor of Ministry Degree from Baptist Bible Seminary in Clark's Summit, Pennsylvania; all as a quadriplegic. It was difficult at times, and even overwhelming at others, but with the help of friends and concerned staff and faculty, God enabled me to persevere. Please don't think that I am being prideful. I thank God for what He has allowed me to accomplished. But I do want to be an encouragement to others who may be wondering if school is an option for them. **GO FOR IT!**

Of course, there still are those daily struggles. I am constantly on the alert for pressure sores, bladder infections, leaky leg bags, and a host of other physical challenges. Just before the Christmas of 1999, I broke my femur (the largest bone in my leg) without realizing it. My leg swelled up and I started getting cold sweats. When I finally went to the hospital to have it checked out, I was as surprised as anyone. That led to more pressure sores, difficulty sleeping, and other unexpected problems. I still get frustrated with curbs, stairs, narrow aisles, and other such inconveniences. In spite of it all, though, God is so good!

God is so good! Appalachian Bible College is indeed a place where God is at work. It has been a gift to me because I know it is a place of such love and caring that I can rest knowing that Jim is there. I thank God for His provision in leading Jim to ABC and for keeping my son and daughter-in-law employed there. My heart is full in thanks to God and to His loving people who continue to serve Him at ABC.

God has been so good to me in other ways also. Jackie married a beautiful Christian man and began a dear little family. They now have three children: Jessica, Boyce and Joanna. JD also married a delightful girl, Tina, whom I love like my own. They also have three children: Macaulie, Aynslie, and Jensen, Jr. John and Karen, his wife and the dearest of daughter-in-laws, have children Jared, Joe, Kristen and Konner. With the addition of all these grandchildren I was so blessed. However, after having a big family around, I was now alone in a big house and very lonesome.

God never stops giving though. He gave me a strong, loving, God-fearing man with whom to share the rest of my life. Stan also was widowed and lonesome but God managed to help us find each other. He has been a blessing in my life and also the lives of my family. He has been the wonderful friend and strong companion that I could lean on. He came with two children, their spouses, and three grandchildren, which made our family pretty big. In a large family there are always crises and Stan has been my support. He's been that large sturdy tree where I can hug and find protection and safety. Best of all, together we know where to go in prayer for all our needs.

Life has a lot of lessons and God uses many different ways to teach them to us. The two most significant lessons I've learned through my experience in this wheelchair have been that God can and wants to use me in my wheelchair, and that I have to be willing to submit my life to Him and follow Him in order to be used as He desires. Since surrendering my life to God, I have found that I have been blessed above and beyond anything that I could ever have imagined. Just like Job, the latter blessings far outnumber the former. God has given me a wonderful wife and daughter (a miracle in itself). I have to tell you about Lindsay. She is the greatest gift that God has ever given to my wife and me. She has brought immeasurable joy into our lives. Even though I can't do all the things that a "regular" Dad does, we still have a lot of fun. She loves to ride on my footrests. She crouches down between my legs and we fly through the mall with reckless abandon, weaving in between the people and laughing all the way. Lindsay is like a chip off the old block when it comes to sports. She loves sports just about as much as I do. Soccer is her favorite, and even though I know nothing about soccer I was her team coach for the last two seasons. I'm sure it was pretty unusual to see a coach in a wheelchair, but we had a great time (and a pretty good season, also, 17–3). There were times after my accident that I thought that none of this would ever be possible; that I would never live a "normal" life. Nothing could be further from the truth! In fact, God has blessed me above measure with more than I could ever want. He has given me a ministry that I love. He has surrounded me with many wonderful friends. He has provided for all of my needs. And he has given me a purpose for living my life in a wheelchair. I am content and my life is full. What more could anyone ask? The following poem sums up my feelings very nicely.

Pressed Out

Pressed out of measure and pressed to all length,
Pressed so intensely it seems beyond strength;
Pressed in the body and pressed in the soul,
Pressed in the mind till the dark surges roll;
Pressure by foes, and pressure by friends,
Pressure on pressure, till life nearly ends,
Pressed into loving the staff and the rod;
Pressed into knowing no helper but God;
Pressed into liberty where nothing clings,
Pressed into faith for impossible things;
Pressed into living a life in the Lord,
Pressed into living a Christ-life outpoured!
—Walter B. Knight

Conclusion

I still go back to the summer place on the island almost every summer. It is still a bittersweet experience. There all my physical limitations are exaggerated and more poignant. There it is harder to get around; everything is more difficult for a wheelchair; doors are smaller, corners are tighter, sidewalks are very uneven, and paths are very bumpy. Everyone has tried to make it easier for me. The ramp now leads to a wide deck and a direct entrance into the cottage. Ramps have been made to get me on and off the ferryboat more easily. Mom had a pontoon boat specially made with wide gates so that my wheelchair can fit through them.

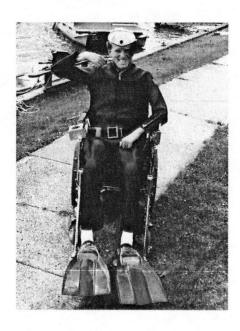

There are many fun times, too. One of the things I enjoy the most is scuba diving. My brother J.D. and I have quite a system worked out. He wears the air tank, a mask, and fins. I wear a mask and weight belts (mainly because I am so buoyant). Then he puts his arm around my waist and holds me to his chest, places a regulator in each of our mouths, and heads for the bottom of the river. We even have signals worked out for me to indicate when I need to clear my ears or if I am in any trouble.

One day we decided to go up the river a little ways and let the current bring us back to our dock. This time I wore a wet suit to keep me warm. It's quite a sight to see a quad in a wet suit with a weight belt, a mask, and fins in a wheelchair. When we got to our destination, J.D. got into the water first. While he waited for me, my mom and my wife, Kathy, laid me down on the edge of the dock, and rolled me in.

As I went under, J.D. caught me, stuck the regulator into my mouth, and down the river we went, not surfacing until we reached our dock. I have often wondered what someone would have thought if they had only seen me getting rolled off the dock. It must have looked like the Mob giving someone a pair of cement shoes. Scuba diving is a lot of fun and one of the most adventurous things that I have done since my accident.

Recently, the Islanders made trails through the woods and for the first time in 20 years, I can get back to the places I loved as a kid. The trails have all been named and the one right behind our cottage has been designated "Jim's Path" because it was especially made so I could follow its winding path back to a platform which looks out over the marshes, canals, and river to the American shore. One can watch the tops of the freighters as they move slowly and majestically through the channel of the St. Clair River. As I take "Jim's Path" to the lookout platform and stare west, I see the Lord's beautiful creation—the sunset, the sparkling water, the birds and wildlife. It's all so serene and perfect, because He is perfect. His will for my life is perfect, too. There is no flaw in His will. In His will is where I want to be for the rest of my life.

What a stark contrast to the scene in the recreation room at the Wisconsin VA! Once, I stared out a window asking, "Why me?" Now, by God's grace, I can stare out over God's creation saying, "Thank you, Lord, for using me!"

We've come a long way along Jim's Path. I find I consider Jim the strongest of all my children. He may not be able to beat his way out of a paper bag, but his strength is not physical. I call him when I need advice of any kind and the rest of the family looks to him for spiritual guidance. We have all grown through his affliction and we've all drawn closer to Christ.

We have all suffered heartache for him and still do on occasion. But still, I wouldn't go back to being the person I was before God changed me, even if it meant Jim's being healed. I know Jim wouldn't have it any other way either. Jim's Path has led us all further along the path God intended for us. All we have to do is look at His perfect creation and we know His way cannot be made any better. His will is perfect. It's where we want to be. Jim's Path will be our path because it is God's path.

A Concise Theology of Suffering

I don't know how many times people have asked me how I can handle things the way I do. I have often wanted to be able to give them something besides quick answers to help them. Having been in a wheelchair now for 20 years and having studied the Scriptures for just about as long, I have come to some conclusions about suffering that I would like to share with you. My thoughts are not exhaustive, but I hope they will be helpful, encouraging, and most of all, will draw you closer to God and His purpose for your life.

I also offer these thoughts because I am burdened about the glut of unbiblical teaching out there concerning suffering and its place in the life of a Christian. From the "Health and Wealth Gospel," which is blatantly unbiblical, to the pulpits of good churches that unintentionally proclaim a message that Christians don't suffer, we have been conditioned to think that suffering is bad and has no part in God's plan for our lives. This fallacy just isn't true. For example, how many times have you heard proclaimed, or said yourself, to an unsaved person, "Accept Jesus as your Savior, and He'll take care of all your problems!" Now, in a certain sense, that's true, but it's also misleading. It makes Jesus sound like a cosmic Santa Claus, who will take all your troubles and trials away. Suffering, though, is an expected part of the believer's life. The sooner we realize that, the sooner we will be more effective in serving our Lord Jesus Christ—more effective in living a Christ-honoring life, more effective and comforting to others who are suffering, and more effective in our witness to the world as they see that we can live in contentment in spite of our circumstances. With this in mind, I will attempt to answer some of the questions that I have been asked. I will seek to answer them biblically and from a personal perspective. I pray that it will be helpful to you.

Why me?

How does a Christian answer this question in reference to suffering or difficult circumstances? Is there any answer? I believe there is and it revolves around understanding who God is and who we are in relationship to Him.

God's Justice and Man's Depravity

The Bible portrays God as a righteous, just, loving, and good God in all of His activities at all times. There are more attributes to God than those listed above, but for our purpose here it is adequate to say that God is at all times righteous, just, loving, and good even in allowing us to suffer the things that we do.

God is righteous and just because He never promised that life would be without suffering. He never obligated Himself to giving us a life of ease. In fact, God would be righteous and just to bring upon us all the fitting consequences of sin in our lives: death and destruction. That's really what we deserve. Paul tells us that in our sinfulness prior to salvation, we "were alienated and enemies" with God (Colossians 1:21). We needed to be reconciled to God. That's one of the reasons why the Lord Jesus Christ suffered for us. But even after salvation, God never promised a life without suffering. In fact, the opposite is true. Look at what Paul said! "Yea, and all that will live godly in Christ Jesus **shall suffer persecution**" (2 Timothy 3:12). Suffering is an expected part of righteous living.

So, do we deserve to suffer at the hands of a righteous and just God? Yes! But because God is loving and gracious, He has withheld the full extent of what we truly deserve. Remember this too. When God allows us to suffer, it is because He has a loving and good purpose behind it.

Suffering Is Universal

When you ask the question, "Why me?" remember that suffering is universal. Everyone suffers. We've all experienced it. It is a part of life. Even those who may not seem to suffer outwardly do have trials and tribulations in their lives. It's part of living in a sin-cursed world. This world is not a perfect place. We are just reaping the consequences of the sin that we and others brought into this world. Often we blame God for our suffering. It's not His fault that we suffer. We've brought it upon ourselves through sin. And thus we have no one to blame to but ourselves.

Suffering Is an Expected Part of the Christian Life

There are a number of Scripture passages that imply that suffering is an expected part of the Christian life. I have already mentioned 2 Timothy 3:12, but there are others. James 1:2–3 says, "My brethren, count it all joy **when** you fall into various trials, knowing this that the testing of your faith produces patience" (NKJ). James doesn't say, "if you fall into various trials," but "when," implying that they are certain to take place in the life of a believer. Peter says, "Beloved, do not think it strange concerning the fiery trial which is to try you, as though some strange thing happened to you; but rejoice to the extent that you partake of Christ's sufferings, that when His glory is revealed, you may also be glad with exceeding joy" (1 Peter 4:12–13 NKJ). Peter expected suffering in the life of a believer. He said that we should not be surprised by it. Paul even indicates that it is a privilege to suffer. Philippians 1:29 says, "For to you it has been granted on behalf of Christ, not only to believe in Him, but also to suffer for His sake." Suffering is not only to be expected, but a biblical perspective suggests that suffering is a privilege for the believer.

Why me? Because of my sinfulness; because suffering is universal; and because it is part of God's plan for all believers.

Why Do We Suffer? God's Rationale for Suffering

After my accident, I often prayed that God would heal me. I thought surely that's what God would want in order to bring glory and honor to His name. I also thought healing me would be the greatest testimony to the grace of God that He could bring to Himself. But, you know what? God did that once by healing the multitudes through our Lord Jesus Christ. He healed them of anything and everything they had. There was nothing that He could not heal. Did they believe? Certainly, some of them did, but the majority of them rejected Him and eventually hung Him on the cross. They came to Him for physical healing, but their hearts were still as diseased and in need of healing as ever. What Christ did physically, man did not allow to happen spiritually! Why does God allow us to suffer? I believe it is because it is the best thing that a loving God could do for us! He wants to heal us spiritually. God's desire is for us to be conformed to the image of His son (Romans 8:28–29), and the best way for Him to accomplish that is through suffering. This is not an exhaustive list, but there are at least six things that God accomplishes in our lives through suffering.

To Prepare Us for Glory

God's planned route for us to glory is through suffering. First Peter 5:10 says, "And after you have suffered for a little while, the God of all grace, who called you to His eternal glory in Christ, will Himself perfect, confirm, strengthen and establish you" (NASB). Eventually, we will be glorified, but God wants to teach us a number of valuable lessons that can only be learned through suffering. Even our Lord Jesus Christ learned through suffering. Hebrews 5:8 says, "Though he were a Son, yet learned he obedience by the things which he suffered." Tribulation is one of God's greatest teachers, and He uses it in our lives to bring us to glory.

To Conform Us to His Son

Another one of the things that God is trying to do through suffering is to conform us to the image of His Son, Jesus Christ. One of the most often quoted verses in times of suffering is Romans 8:28. "And we know that all things work together for good to them that love God, to them who are the called according to *his* purpose." We quote it, only half believing that what we're going through really is for good. We sometimes wonder what possible good could ever come from this adversity. But when we put Romans 8:29 with the preceding verse, we find Paul's explanation of God's purpose. "For whom he did foreknow, he also did predestinate *to be* conformed to the image of his Son, that he might be the firstborn among many brethren." All things work together for good because they are intended to conform us to the image of Jesus Christ. Whether they be blessings, or trials and tribulations, God wants to use them to conform us to Christ; and that's good.

God also uses discipline to conform us to the image of His Son. Hebrews tells us that God disciplines His children. He does it for two reasons. First, to profit us (12:10), and second, that we might yield the peaceable fruit of righteousness (vs. 11). God uses chastening in our lives to weed out the evil and build godly character. Sometimes the reason we suffer is that God is not pleased with our conduct. God uses chastening to get our attention and draw us back into conformity to His Son. It may not be pleasant for the moment, but God uses it to accomplish His purpose in our lives. In my own personal experience, I believe that God was chastening me to a certain degree. I was stubbornly headed in the direction that I wanted to go, conveniently asking God to bless my plans. Through my accident, God got my attention and redirected my life. Had it not been for the chastening of the Lord, I would never have found God's true purpose for my life. I'm quite confident that I would never have surrendered my life to full-time Christian service without God's chastening. I am thankful that God did chasten me and redirected my attention toward His will. I am happier today serving the Lord Jesus Christ in my wheelchair than I ever would have been serving myself and my own aspirations for life.

To Learn Submission

First Peter 2:13–3:7 is all about submission. Peter says that we are to submit ourselves "to every ordinance of man for the Lord's sake" (2:13). He says that servants are to submit to their masters (vs. 18). He says that wives are to submit to their husbands (3:1) and that husbands are to submit to their wives by showing them respect (vs. 7). Right in the middle of this discourse on submission, Peter draws our attention to the Lord Jesus Christ.

"For even hereunto were ye called: because Christ also suffered for us, leaving us an example, that ye should follow his steps: Who did no sin, neither was guile found in his mouth: Who, when he was reviled, reviled not again;

when he suffered, he threatened not; but committed *himself* to him that judgeth righteously: Who his own self bare our sins in his own body on the tree, that we, being dead to sins, should live unto righteousness: by whose stripes ye were healed" (1 Peter 2:21–24).

Peter says that Christ is our example in submission. Just as Christ submitted Himself to the Father and suffered the shame and disgrace of the cross, likewise we are to submit ourselves to those who are in authority over us, whether it involves suffering or not. Jesus Christ is our example. Jesus could have retaliated while He was on the cross suffering, but He didn't. He could have called upon a legion of angels to wipe out His enemies. Instead, He submitted Himself to the Father's will. Peter says that we are called to do likewise. Suffering gives us the opportunity to demonstrate that we have learned to be submissive to the Father's will.

To Keep Us Humble

God uses suffering to keep us humble. Paul is an excellent illustration of this in 2 Corinthians 12:1–10. In that passage, where Paul is defending his apostolic authority, he starts to describe for us some of the tremendous visions he was privileged to receive. His natural tendency would have been to brag about such incredible blessings, but God sent him a thorn in the flesh to keep him humble. Paul says, "And lest I should be exalted above measure through the abundance of the revelations, there was given to me a thorn in the flesh, the messenger of Satan to buffet me, lest I should be exalted above measure" (2 Corinthians 12:7). What the thorn in the flesh was, we can't be sure. But whatever it was it had to do with suffering to the degree that Paul sought earnestly to get rid of it. The fact that his thorn in the flesh is unidentifiable is really a blessing. Because it is generic, we can all identify. We all know what it's like to suffer and pray that God would remove the suffering. But because God blesses us tremendously, and because He doesn't want us to get puffed up thinking we deserve those blessings based on our own merit or goodness, He uses suffering to keep us humble.

To Comfort Others

"Blessed *be* God, even the Father of our Lord Jesus Christ, the Father of mercies, and the God of all comfort; Who comforteth us in all our tribulation, that we may be able to comfort them which are in any trouble, by the comfort wherewith we ourselves are comforted of God" (2 Corinthians 1:3–4).

God allows us to suffer so that we might be able to comfort others who suffer also. God wants us to be ministers of His grace and peace. He wants us to use our experiences to be a blessing to others. Look around you. The world is full of hurting people! They have no idea where to turn for relief and comfort. The world offers no hope for them. But we have hope! We have experienced it! God wants us to share with others so that they might experience God's grace in their lives. Who knows, you may be the only one who can give some hurting soul a glimpse of the wonderful grace of God. What a privilege it is to carry on the very work that God has performed in our lives. He has comforted us, now it is our turn to comfort others.

God emphatically illustrated this principle in my life when I was just a sophomore at Appalachian Bible College.

I was home for Thanksgiving break and mom told me about some friends who were really struggling. The husband of this couple was driving home from work one evening when he was in an accident and broke his neck. Whenever I hear about these kinds of things it immediately brings a flood of memories and emotions to my mind. Mom said that they were having a very difficult time understanding why God would let this happen to them. The Lord impressed upon me the need to go and visit. My intent was just to be an encouragement. I figured that I would only be there about 30 minutes because I wasn't sure if they were emotionally ready yet to receive handicapped visitors. As soon as I arrived they welcomed me with open arms, and immediately I was bombarded with the "Why Me?" questions. I knew that these folks were not saved, so I began to tell them my testimony. I told them how Jesus Christ was my personal savior, and that he was working very intimately in my life. I reviewed for them how I had struggled with the same questions, and how Christ eventually brought me to an understanding of His will for my life. I told them that Jesus could do the same thing for them. A 30-minute visit soon turned into three hours, two salvation decisions, and a whole lot of joy and tears. After I left, God impressed me with 2 Corinthians 1:3–4. I was used to comfort others with the same comfort that God used to comfort me. What a joy that experience was! Even if that was all God intended to do through me in my wheelchair, it was worth it.

To Be a Witness to the World

First Peter 3:15 is often used to exhort Christians to be ready at any time to either witness to others or, in the case of Christian workers, to be ready to preach at any time. We are to be ready at any time to witness for our faith. Some preachers have for a motto, "Be Ready to Preach, Pray, or Perish!" Unfortunately, though this is a needed exhortation and is a necessary exercise for the growth of the Church, it is a misuse of this verse. As we look at 1 Peter 3:15, it is important to discover how it fits into the flow of Peter's thoughts throughout the Epistle. Once we have identified how it fits in the whole Book, we can then seek to understand what Peter intended when he said, "But sanctify the Lord God in your hearts: and be ready always to give an answer to every man that asketh you a reason of the hope that is in you with meekness and fear" (1 Peter 3:15).

The theme of 1 Peter is "Suffering in Submission." This can be seen in the key verse, 1 Peter 2:21, in which Peter calls the Jews of the Dispersion in the regions of Cappadocia and Galatia to submit themselves to suffering as exemplified by Jesus Christ. Just as Jesus submitted Himself to the suffering of the cross, Peter's readers should submit themselves to suffering for the sake of a good testimony for Jesus Christ. It is probable that these readers were subject to suffering many different things from the ungodly people who inhabited the regions of Cappadocia and Galatia. Nero was just beginning his horrendous persecution of Christians by throwing them to the lions or by burning them on crosses to light his garden parties. Just living beyond the borders of Jerusalem and Judea brought persecution and suffering to the Jews. Their suffering was intensified by the fact that these Jews were also Christians. They were persecuted by the ungodly Gentiles and by the zealous Judaizers. Peter's intent was to comfort the Jews in the midst of suffering for

Christ, and to encourage them to continue in submission to the will of God.

We can easily see the progression of this theme in the flow of the epistle. Peter starts by showing his audience that the ultimate end of suffering will be salvation (1:3–1:12). This salvation is characterized by the glorious resurrection of Jesus Christ and the hope of joy inexpressible that is anticipated by all believers, though for a short time they are grieved by various trials. Peter encourages his readers to rejoice in spite of adversity. It will be worth it in the end.

Next, Peter exhorts his readers to live godly lives regardless of the difficult circumstances surrounding them. He reminds them that they are called to be holy, just as God is holy, and that they have the resource of the Word of God to guide and direct them into holiness (1:13–2:12). The end result will be that unbelievers will glorify God. This in itself is sufficient to cause believers to submit to suffering, but also because they are called of God to be His people, they are commanded to "proclaim the praises of Him who called you out of darkness into His marvelous light" (1 Peter 2:9 NKJ). Holy living is possible, even in the midst of suffering. It is our holy conduct in suffering that brings glory and honor to God the Father.

From 1 Peter 2:13 to 1 Peter 3:12, Peter deals with submission in our earthly relationships. He highlights submission to government, masters, wives, husbands, and to one another. It is in this context that Peter says we may suffer for properly submitting to those who are in authority over us, and that this kind of suffering is commendable before God. God is pleased when we suffer for doing good, but there is no commendation for suffering for doing evil. We deserve to suffer if we are involved in evil activities, but God is pleased if we suffer for doing good.

Next Peter turns to the will of God in suffering. It may be God's will for His people to suffer. That should not surprise us. God has a purpose for suffering righteously. Suffering in submission for righteousness' sake will result in a good conscience before God. Peter exhorts his readers to forsake their fleshly past because it will ultimately bring permanent suffering and judgment. The proper response to difficult trials and to one another is to have fervent love, which covers a multitude of sins, and to minister to one another's needs according to the gifts that God has given to each of us (3:13–4:19). There is strength and support among family members that will help us in times of adversity. There is also the knowledge of the sovereignty of God. He is ultimately in control of all that touches our lives. Peter encourages his readers to be confident in the Lord.

It is in this context that Peter encourages his readers to be ready to give an answer to every man. He says that they will sometimes suffer for righteousness' sake, but that they should not be afraid of the threats of ungodly men. Apparently Peter has in mind that his readers were suffering at the hands of ungodly men for doing what is good. It is at these times that they can have a good testimony for the Lord, so he encourages them to do two things. First, he commands them to sanctify the Lord God in their hearts. The word "sanctify" means to set apart. They were to set apart the Lord God in their hearts. He wanted them to concentrate wholly and solely on God for strength and direction in these difficult times. God is the only One who will give them the strength to endure suffering in a way that will bring glory to the Lord God Almighty.

Second, he commands them to be ready to give a defense for the hope that is in them. This hope reverts back to 1 Peter 1:3–4 where Peter describes the living hope of resurrection in Jesus Christ which is an inheritance incorruptible and undefiled and that does not fade away. It is this hope that Peter exhorts them to proclaim. It is also this hope that will help them endure suffering in this life. The author of the book of Hebrews said that we are to run the race of life with perseverance by "looking onto Jesus, the author and finisher of our faith, who for the joy that was set before him endured the cross, despising the shame, and is set down at the right hand of the throne of God" (Hebrews 12:1–2). Christ is our example of looking ahead to the hope awaiting us to help us persevere in adversity. So, as they exhibit a good testimony before ungodly men in the midst of suffering, Peter encourages them to use it as an opportunity to explain to those who ask the reason that they can rejoice. This life's suffering is only temporary, and believers in Christ have the hope of a future resurrection that will be characterized by inexpressible joy. "For our light affliction, which is but for a moment, worketh for us a far more exceeding and eternal weight of glory" (2 Corinthians 4:17).

Peter closes his epistle of encouragement with another round of exhortation (5:1–5:11). He reminds the elders to be good examples of submission in suffering, and the young men to exercise submission to the elders. It is only at the end of the epistle that Peter indicates one of the key ingredients to submission in suffering. That ingredient is humility. Peter commands his readers to humble themselves before

God. God is sovereign. God knows what He is doing, even when He allows suffering in the lives of His people. Ultimately, it is the work of God to bring glory to His Name through suffering. We must humble ourselves before Him and allow Him to accomplish His work, the work of conforming us to the image of His Son and the work of being a witness to the world of His grace.

As I said before, this is not an exhaustive list, but it is sufficient to show us that God uses suffering in our lives for many different good reasons. The works that God desires to accomplish in our lives through suffering bring joy, peace, contentment, and fulfillment. God's ways are not our ways. He is "able to do exceeding abundantly above all that we ask or think, according to the power that worketh in us" (Ephesians 3:20). Our responsibility is to humbly submit ourselves to His work.

How Do I Handle Suffering?

God's Grace

My life verse is "And he said unto me, My grace is sufficient for thee: for my strength is made perfect in weakness. Most gladly therefore will I rather glory in my infirmities, that the power of Christ may rest upon me. Therefore I take pleasure in infirmities, in reproaches, in necessities, in persecutions, in distresses for Christ's sake: for when I am weak, then am I strong" (2 Corinthians 12:9). Just prior to this statement Paul had prayed to the Lord three times asking that his thorn in the flesh be removed. But God said, "No!" Can you imagine? If anyone deserved to be healed,

Paul did. Paul was sold out for the Lord. In fact, he was used of God to bring healing to others (Acts 14:8–10); why shouldn't he expect to be healed himself? But God had something better for Paul. It was His grace, and Paul realized it too! He realized that God's grace resulted in a marvelous provision for his life. God's strength was made perfect in Paul's weakness. It was because of this fact that Paul gloried in his infirmities. He realized that by doing so, the power of Christ rested upon him. That's a pretty significant power when you consider that Jesus Christ created the universe and everything in it (John 1:3; Colossians 1:16; Hebrews 1:2). The same power that Jesus Christ used to heal the paralytic, to cause the blind to see, to raise Lazarus from the dead, and to conquer death, was the power that was now abiding on Paul as he gloried in his thorn in the flesh. With that kind of power at his disposal, Paul could overcome any of the difficulties that his infirmities presented. Was God's grace sufficient for Paul? Absolutely, yes! Is God's grace sufficient for our trials? Absolutely, yes! Paul realized that through his weakness, he was made strong—not with his own strength, but with God's. By God's grace, Paul's weaknesses were turned into opportunities for God to manifest His strength. That's why Paul took pleasure in infirmities, reproaches, necessities, persecutions, and distresses. God manifested His strength through Paul's weaknesses to bring glory to His Name.

People often ask me how I can be content with my life in a wheelchair. The answer is easy! God's grace is sufficient for me too, and by His grace, He manifests His strength through my weaknesses. What a privilege it is to have the power of Christ resting upon me! What a tremendous opportunity to be a testimony of God's grace to the world!

God Knows Our Limits

"There hath no temptation taken you but such as is common to man: but God *is* faithful, who will not suffer you to be tempted above that ye are able; but will with the temptation also make a way to escape, that ye may be able to bear *it*" (1 Corinthians 10:13). There are times when the struggles of suffering seem so overwhelming that we want to throw up our hands and say, "I just can't take it anymore! I quit!" It surely is a comfort to know that we are not alone in our temptations. God knows our limits. There is a sense of reassurance in knowing that others have faced the same things that I am facing and have been victorious in them. Even Jesus Christ knows the temptations that I am facing (Hebrews 2:18; 4:15). The testimony of others who have gone before me and have been victorious in the same kinds of temptations that I'm facing, is an encouragement to me that I also can be victorious. It's also encouraging to know that He knows what we can and cannot take. He knows the point at which the temptations we are experiencing will overwhelm us, and He promises that He will not permit the temptations to be more than we are able to handle. He always provides a way to escape and to bear up under the pressure of falling to the temptation. The key is recognizing what we've discussed above. As we learn to appropriate God's grace in our lives, we will escape the temptation and we will be able to bear whatever circumstances are trying us. And not only will we be able to bear it, but we will be able to glorify God through it. Isn't God's grace marvelous?

An Attitude of Gratitude Makes the Difference

"For I reckon that the sufferings of this present time are not worthy to be compared with the glory which shall be revealed in us" (Romans 8:18).

Attitude is everything! An attitude of gratitude can make all the difference in the world. Paul demonstrated that kind of attitude a number of different times. In the verse above, he summarizes his feelings about suffering and hardships. He concludes that all the suffering of this life cannot even be compared to the glory that awaits us in heaven. Now remember, Paul understood what it meant to suffer. Second Corinthians 11:23–28 gives us a whole list of things that Paul suffered, both physical and emotional. One of the most amazing testimonies of Paul's attitude in the midst of suffering is found in the Book of Philippians, which was written from a prison cell. The theme of the book is "Joy in the Christian Life." Philippians 4:4 sums up Paul's whole attitude toward hardship. He says, "Rejoice in the Lord alway: and again I say, rejoice." Further on in that chapter, Paul talks about how he learned to be content in whatever state he found himself. He said, "I know how to get along with humble means, and I also know how to live in prosperity; in any and every circumstance I have learned the secret of being filled and going hungry, both of having abundance and suffering need" (vs. 12, NASB). What's his secret? Jesus Christ! In Philippians 4:13, Paul says, "I can do all things through Him who strengthens me" (NASB). As we draw close to Jesus Christ with an attitude of gratitude, He enables us to handle whatever hardships life brings our way.

James also had an attitude of gratitude. He said, "My brethren, count it all joy when you fall into various trials, knowing this, that the testing of your faith produces patience. But let patience have *its* perfect work, that you may be perfect and complete, lacking nothing" (James 1:2–4 NKJ). James recognized that one of the benefits of suffering was the building of patience into the life of a believer. It was the work of suffering that accomplished maturity in the believer. Because of that, James said to reckon suffering a joyful thing. He had an attitude of gratitude. Paul said that one evidence of being controlled by the Holy Spirit is thankfulness (Ephesians 5:20). He said, "In everything give thanks; for this is the will of God in Christ Jesus for you" (1 Thessalonians 5:18). I know that that is difficult to do! Believe me, there are times when I still struggle with being thankful for my wheelchair, but God's Word commands that I be thankful. I cannot get around that. Therefore, I must make a conscious choice to be thankful for the circumstances of my life.

Consider also the benefits of suffering, as we have already described above. Suffering prepares us for glory (1 Peter 5:10), conforms us to the image of our Lord Jesus Christ (Romans 8:28–29; Hebrews 12), teaches us submission (Hebrews 5:8), and keeps us humble (2 Corinthians 12). The benefits of suffering through adversity far outweigh the losses in this life. Paul said, "For our light affliction, which is but for a moment, worketh for us a far more exceeding and eternal weight of glory" (2 Corinthians 4:16). Not only does suffering benefit us in the here and now, but it also benefits us in eternity.

The bottom line here is that your attitude toward suffering is a choice. You can choose to be angry at God. You can choose to rebel, run, and resist God's work in your life, or you can submit yourself to His will and allow Him to accomplish the work He desires to accomplish in your life. You can choose to serve God. You can choose to avail yourself to the benefits of suffering: benefits in this life and the life to come. The choice is yours. The world says, "Resist!" God says, "Be blessed!" Joshua said, "And if it seems evil to you to serve the LORD, choose for yourselves this day whom you will serve, whether the gods which your fathers served that *were* on the other side of the River, or the gods of the Amorites, in whose land you dwell. But as for me and my house, we will serve the LORD" (Joshua 24:15 NKJ). Whom will you serve?

Now, I know it's not always easy to have a good attitude toward adversity. Believe me, there are still times that I get very frustrated and angry because I'm in a wheelchair. Curbs, narrow doors, having to wait outside in the cold winter weather for someone to open the door, are just the daily challenges of life to overcome. Some of the more difficult things have to do with my daughter. I would love to be able to teach her how to throw a ball, ride her bike, or dive into the water, but I can't. But I can still spend time with her, giving her rides on my lap, or racing her up and down the sidewalk. With the proper attitude there are always things for which to be grateful.

Being confined to wheelchair is never boring either. I've gotten myself into a number of situations that were less than ideal. One beautiful summer day while we were vacationing on the island, I decided to take a walk (not a wheel or a roll, I go for walks just like everyone else). I went by myself just to spend some time alone. I decided to take one of the trails through the woods. It led back to some of the places that I used to go to when I was a kid. It was relatively flat and level, so I didn't think I would have any problems. If it hadn't been for that divot in the ground, I would have been just fine. My left front wheel caught the divot and my body launched forward as my chair stopped. Fortunately, the wheelchair didn't tip over, but I did, and I couldn't get back into an upright sitting position. There I was in the middle of the woods, way off the beaten path, and no one had any idea where I was. Well, I knew someone would eventually miss me and come looking, but I wasn't sure I wanted to wait that long. I prayed to God and said, "Lord, I could really use some help right now. I would be mighty appreciative if You would bring someone my way." I decided to swallow my pride and start screaming for help. I can't scream very loud, but I did the best I could for about five minutes. It seemed like much longer. I didn't even really expect anyone to hear me, but, low and behold, I got a faint reply. Someone hollered back, "Do you really need help or are you just playing?" My reply was emphatic, "I've fallen and I can't get up!" After I was rescued, I went straight home a little shaken up, but very grateful for God's provision. Later on that day, I found out that some other people had also heard my cries for help. They said that they were not sure whether they heard a person or a dying raccoon. I wasn't very flattered.

Equipment breakdowns are also frustrating, and sometimes life-threatening. This is really true in the mountains of West Virginia. One evening, I was going down the hill from the men's dorm at ABC to the cafeteria for dinner. One of the drive belts on my wheelchair slipped off and my chair started careening down the hill out of control. I couldn't do anything but go along for the ride. I kept going faster and faster, and eventually went off the side of the road and down a steep incline. At the bottom I came to a sudden stop. I fell over forward but fortunately, because I had my seat belt on, I stayed in the chair. The footrest on my wheel-chair broke, but other than that I was fine. My wife (who was my girlfriend at the time) saw the whole thing from her dorm room window. Before she could reach me, a whole mob of fellow students had come to the rescue. Physically I was fine, but emotionally my pride was bruised and I was embarrassed.

These incidences and many more like them make life in a wheelchair very interesting and challenging. I have to stay close to God. It is vital for me to tap into His strength and grace daily. It is only by keeping an eternal and godly per-spective that I am able to handle living life confined to a wheelchair. But, God has been so good to me! And I am exceedingly grateful that He is my Lord and Savior. An atti-tude of gratitude makes all the different in the world!

What about Healing?

God Can Heal

What about healing? Can God heal today? I've been asked that question many times, and have asked it myself. The answer is, yes! God can heal. He is our creator and He is omnipotent. There is plenty of evidence in the Bible that God is able to heal. The question is not whether He is able, but rather, is that His will? Many people say that it is God's will to heal His children in our age. They say, "Jesus is the same yesterday, today, and forever. And since He healed people in the Gospels, He is obligated to heal today." This sounds good, but it doesn't take into consideration the context of the verse cited above from Hebrews, nor the whole scope of healing in the Bible. Is it God's will to heal today? Consider some of the following thoughts.

Biblical History of Healing

First, let's look at the history of healing in the Bible. For the most part, healing is confined to the ministry of our Lord Jesus Christ. In the Old Testament, which consists of writings that span a history of over at least 4000 years, there are very few instances of healing recorded. Miriam was healed of leprosy (Numbers 12:10–15). Moses was commanded by God to make a bronze serpent and lift it up on a pole. When the people who had been bitten by a snake looked upon it they were healed (Numbers 21:7–8). King Hezekiah was healed and given a 15-year extension on his life (2 Kings 20:5–6). Naaman, the Gentile general of the Syrian army, was also healed of leprosy (2 Kings 5:1–15). But, other than that, healings are very few and far between. When we look at the history of the Bible after the life of our Lord Jesus Christ and the ministry of His apostles during the inaugural years of the church, the same is true. Healings are very few and far between. Granted, the apostles were involved in a healing ministry during the early chapters of the Book of Acts, but that fades off the scene quite suddenly, and by the end of the book it has almost completely disappeared. There was only one time in all of history when there was an intense outbreak of healing, and that was during the ministry of our Lord Jesus Christ, a period of approximately 3 1/2 years.

Biblical Purpose of Healing

Second, let's look at the purpose for the intense ministry of healing by Jesus Christ. Jesus pointed people to him through his healing. He was the Messiah. The Old Testament predicted that the Messiah would bring healing to the nation of Israel (Psalm 103:3; Isaiah 29:18; 32:3; 35:5–6; cf. also Zephaniah 3:19). Jesus did exactly that (Matthew 4:23; 9:35). He preached the kingdom message and performed the kingdom works, and did so to prove to the nation that He was the Messiah. So, the miracles that Jesus did, including healing, were done to authenticate Him as the Messiah (Matthew 11:4–5). After He was rejected and crucified, His messianic kingdom was postponed until His Second Coming. Thus, there was no longer any need for authenticating miracles.

The miracles, including healings that are recorded in the early chapters of the book of Acts, were also given for the purpose of authentication. In this case, it was the authentication of the church. The Jews, who had been steeped in the Law of Moses for nearly 1500 years, naturally had a very hard time accepting the fact that God was going to work through a new establishment, the Church. God made it abundantly clear that He was doing a new work through the miracles of His apostles. Once the church was established, the authenticating miracles no longer were needed. Thus, we have a very simple and logical explanation for why the ministry of healing no longer exists. There is no need to authenticate the work of the church or the Messiahship of Jesus Christ.

So, can God heal today? Yes, but this is generally the exception to the rule. Because God no longer has a need to authenticate the church, and because He has chosen to use suffering and adversity to cause us to grow in Christ, it is normally not His will to heal His children.

Biblical Characteristics of Healing

There's one more question that I think bears consideration. What about miracle workers, or the gift of healing? Does such a gift exist today? Well, there are a number of good books on the subject already in print. My purpose here is not to give a definitive answer to the question, but to cast doubt and skepticism on the practices that are common today in the realm of healing services. It is my pet peeve because I have seen so many young believers devastated by the hope of obtaining a miracle. There are two things that I would like to say here. First, when Jesus Christ healed someone it was never based upon having sufficient faith. It was only based upon belief in who He was. Christ never said to anyone, "You don't have enough faith to be healed." In fact, many times Christ's miracles promoted greater faith and belief (Matthew 8:26; 9:22; Mark 9:24; 10:52). Contrary to what Christ was trying to accomplish through miracles, today we have healing services that devastate faith. When someone goes to a miracle worker for healing and a miracle is denied, the common explanation is that the seeker does not have enough faith. If his faith was great enough, he would have received his miracle. I was once told that if I have enough faith, God would heal me. I had all the faith in the world that God could heal me, but He didn't. Why? Was it because my faith wasn't great enough? I thought I had enough, but according to those who believe in the "Name It and Claim It" theology, I didn't. Well, I was fortunate to have many friends around me who could give me sound biblical explanations and advice. But my heart goes out to those who have been devastated because they have been told that they have insufficient faith. What are they to do to build their faith? I have yet to hear a good answer.

Second, I would like to just give a concise description of the characteristics of Christ's healings, in contrast to the characteristics of the types of healing that are typical today. Christ's miracles almost always had the following attributes:

They were instantaneous (Mark 1:42).

They were complete (Matthew 14:35–36).

They were permanent (Matthew 14:35–36);

They were concerned with physical disorders (leprosy - Mark 1:40, deformities - Luke 6:6) and not psychological illnesses or habits, such as drinking or smoking;

They were secondary to the preaching of the Word of God (Luke 9:6).

They were always successful, even when the disciples failed (Matthew 17:20).

Consider, just for instance, the complexity involved in healing the lame man at the Pool of Bethesda (John 5). After having been lame for 38 years, he would suffer not only from the neurological disorders, but also atrophied muscles, brittle bones, lack of coordination, the inability to stand without fainting, and a myriad of other physical problems that would have to be overcome in order to walk again. But when

Jesus healed the lame man, all of these problems were immediately solved. Scripture says, "Jesus saith unto him, Rise, take up thy bed, and walk. And immediately the man was made whole, and took up his bed, and walked: and on the same day was the sabbath" (John 5:8–9). There was no evidence that the man had ever been paralyzed. He was immediately made completely whole. He walked and jumped with body parts that were fully developed and mature physically. The complexity of physical problems that had to be overcome in this one miracle is mind-boggling, but Jesus Christ did it.

It should be noted that there are two miracles performed by our Lord Jesus Christ that were not instantaneous. The first is Mark 8:23, where Jesus restored a blind man's sight only partially at first, and then completely. The second is John 9:6, where Jesus anointed another blind man's eyes with clay and spittle and then sent him to the Pool of Siloam to wash his eyes, at which time his sight was restored. In both cases, one of the purposes for the delay in healing was to encourage the faith of the recipient of the miracle, not because Christ couldn't perform the miracle immediately, nor because the recipient had insufficient faith.

Note also that the multitudes went to Jesus because His fame spread throughout the region. Matthew reports, "And Jesus went about all Galilee, teaching in their synagogues, and preaching the gospel of the kingdom, and healing all manner of sickness and all manner of disease among the people. And his fame went throughout all Syria: and they brought unto him all sick people that were taken with divers diseases and torments, and those which were possessed with devils, and those which were lunatick, and those that had the palsy; and he healed them" (Matthew 4:23–24). You can't help but be impressed with the all-inclusive nature of Christ's healing ministry. He went about **all** Galilee. He healed **all** manner of sickness and **all** manner of disease. His fame went throughout **all** Syria. They brought unto him **all** sick people. And, He healed them, every one! Mark testifies, "Wherever He entered into villages, cities, or in the country, they laid the sick in the marketplaces, and begged Him that they might just touch the hem of His garment. And as many as touched Him were made well" (Mark 6:56 NKJ). Now, compare that with miracle workers today. There is obviously quite a discrepancy.

My point is this: What we see today being done by miracle workers and those who claim to have to gift of healing is not at all like what was done by our Lord Jesus Christ or by His apostles. In fact, they are so diverse that it is doubtful that the miracle workers of today are legitimate at all. They aren't. They offer hope, but destroy faith, and by so doing, discourage people from following the will of God.

Conclusion

As you can see, the Bible clearly teaches that suffering is a part of the Christian life. We suffer adversity because of the results of sin in our lives and in the world. We suffer adversity because God is purposefully working to conform us to the image of our Lord Jesus Christ. We suffer adversity because God wants to use us to comfort others and be a testimony to the world. We shouldn't be surprised when we're faced with hardships, as if it is something that is foreign to the believer's walk. Instead, we should embrace adversity, submit ourselves humbly to it, learn from it, and seek to glorify God through it. Only then will we truly enjoy life as it was meant to be, full of peace, joy, and contentment.

To order additional copies of

Jim's Path

Please visit our web site at
www.pleasantword.com

Also available at: www.amazon.com